Political Accountability and European Integration

Europa Law Publishing, Groningen 2009

Political Accountability and European Integration

Edited by Luc Verhey, Philipp Kiiver & Sandor Loeffen

Europa Law Publishing is a publishing company specializing in European Union law, international trade law, public international law, environmental law and comparative national law.
For further information please contact Europa Law Publishing via email: info@europalawpublishing.com or visit our website at: www.europalawpublishing.com.

Typeset in Scala and Scala Sans, Graphic design by G2K Designers, Groningen/Amsterdam

NUR 828; ISBN 978-90-8952-055-5

Authors

Thomas Christiansen
Senior Lecturer, European Institute of Public Administration

Paul Craig
Professor of English Law, University of Oxford

Deirdre Curtin
Professor of European Law, University of Amsterdam and Professor of International and European Governance, University of Utrecht

Jan Jacob van Dijk
Chair, Joint Committee on the Review of Subsidiarity, Dutch Parliament

Walter van Gerven
Professor of Law, University of Leuven

Sandor Loeffen
Researcher, Department of Public Law, Maastricht University

Philipp Kiiver
Associate Professor of European and Comparative Constitutional Law, Maastricht University

Veith Mehde
Professor of Public Law, Leibniz University Hannover

Dawn Oliver
Professor of Constitutional Law, University College London

Jit Peters
Professor of Constitutional and Administrative Law, University of Amsterdam

Michael Shackleton
Project Manager and Head of Unit, European Parliament Secretariat

Luc Verhey
Professor of Constitutional and Administrative Law, Maastricht University, and Director of the Maastricht branch of the Montesquieu Institute

Anchrit Wille
Senior Researcher, Utrecht University

Bruno de Witte
Professor of European Union Law, European University Institute Florence

CHAPTER I

Introduction

Luc Verhey, Philipp Kiiver, Sandor Loeffen

1 Introduction

This collection is based on the contributions to the final conference of the SaRO research programme on political control and accountability in a European and comparative perspective, which took place in Maastricht in March 2008. The programme was set up in 2004 by the universities of Maastricht, Utrecht and Amsterdam within the framework of the Ius Commune research school and funded by a research grant of the Netherlands Organisation for Scientific Research (NWO). The main objective of the programme was to develop principles and create ideas for the organisation of political control and accountability in the future European Union. It has been carried out by three research groups, which were under the direction of Luc Verhey (Professor of Constitutional and Administrative Law, Maastricht University), Deirdre Curtin (Professor of International and European Governance, Utrecht University and, as of September 2008, Professor of European Law, University of Amsterdam) and Jit Peters (Professor of Constitutional Law, University of Amsterdam).

The book is published under the responsibility of the Maastricht branch of the Montesquieu Institute, the Centre of European Parliamentary History and Constitutional Development. The Montesquieu Institute is an inter-university initiative, dedicated to stimulating the comparative and interdisciplinary study of parliaments and parliamentary government in Europe. In bringing together academic researchers of different disciplines as well as practitioners to discuss the subject of political accountability in the context of European integration, this book illustrates what the Montesquieu Institute has set out to achieve.

2 Background: A *'Ius Commune'* of Political Accountability

The SaRO research project on political accountability has been developed in the context of the Ius Commune research school. The research school focuses on the interaction between international, European and national legal systems. This multi-level interaction is studied from two perspectives. The first is to analyse the influence of international integration developments, especially the European integration process, on national legal and constitutional orders. This includes questions regarding the unification and harmonisation of national legal norms and traditions. The second direction is to identify common principles which have been developed in different national legal systems over time ('ius commune') and to analyse if and how processes of international and European integration can be built upon these common principles. The 'ius commune' approach to legal research is, therefore, a two-way approach which works top-down (how does international and European integration affect national legal systems?) and bottom-up (how national do legal systems affect international and European integration?).

This way of looking at international and European integration processes has consequences for the method of research. Research from a 'ius commune' point of view cannot be limited to a study of international processes, nor can it merely approach a subject from a strictly national perspective. Both European and comparative research are required. In this research project, we have tried to bring together both European and national oriented academics, not only lawyers, but also experts in the fields of political science and public administration in order to ensure that all relevant perspectives are taken into account.

Against this background, this research project is an attempt to apply the 'ius commune' approach to the concept of accountability, with a special focus on the process of European integration. The issue of accountability is often seen as being closely related to debates on democracy, both at the European and the national level. At the European Union level, the rejection of the Constitutional Treaty by France and the Netherlands, followed by the Irish no to the Lisbon Treaty, seems to have made it more and more urgent to think about improving accountability processes as one of the paths towards reducing the gap between the European Union and its citizens. What is unclear, however, is how to achieve this.

3 Understanding Accountability: A Comparative Approach

In analysing the concept of accountability, different starting points are available. Given the aforementioned parallel between the accountability and democracy debates, the Lisbon Treaty offers a helpful framework where it distinguishes between two forms of democracy: representative and participatory democracy. The concept of accountability can be approached along similar lines. The traditional approach to political accountability in many European legal systems is founded on the notion of representative democracy, that is, political accountability or responsibility of the executive towards a parliament. In this context, accountability is seen as the right of the parliament to be informed by the government which gives account of its actions and, where appropriate, suffers the consequences, takes the blame or undertakes to put matters right if it should appear that errors have been made.

Accountability can also be seen in a broader sense, where it is understood as including the giving of account more directly to the people. Here, the concept of accountability is closely related to principle of participatory democracy. In this context, executive institutions are expected to inform the public about their achievements and consult with interest groups about proposed policies or actions. In this sense, accountability is not limited to the parliamentary context, but involves civil society or the public. An example of such a broad definition can be found in the European Commission's White Paper of 2001, which declared 'accountability' as one of the principles that underpin 'good governance' in Europe.[1] The White Paper referred to accountability in a general sense as the obligation of EU institutions 'to explain and take responsibility for what it does in Europe'. This definition includes giving account to parliaments, but it is much more than that.

At this abstract level, the European Union approach is not fundamentally different from the perspective in at least some of its Member States. In the Netherlands, for example, the debate about accountability is essentially on how to strike a balance between political accountability on the one hand and alternative forms of accountability on the other. While the traditional mechanisms of political accountability are still considered to be of crucial importance, this debate has, so far, indicated that they have become less self-evident.

National discussions cannot easily be viewed separately from the debate on accountability in the European Union. On the contrary, one of the assumptions of this research project has been that the accountability deficit in the European Union cannot be solved effectively unless European rules and mechanisms are firmly rooted in the longstanding constitutional traditions of the Member States. Article 6 of the EU Treaty also notes the interrelation of European and national legal principles and theories, where it states that the European Union is founded on the principles of freedom, democracy, human rights and the rule of law which 'the Member States have in common.' The difficulty is, of course, how to translate these common national principles in practice into sound constitutional provisions at the European level.

4 The Research Framework

Since the concept of accountability can take many forms and shapes, the scope of the research project had to be limited to manageable proportions. Therefore, the project was divided in three subprojects, each focusing on a specific aspect of accountability in the European context.

The first subproject, carried out by the University of Amsterdam, concerns national parliamentary control of EU decision making. The purpose of this study was to contribute to the development of a comprehensive regime of national parliamentary control on the basis of a comparative analysis of scrutiny systems, as they exist today in the Member States. This study has resulted in a volume edited by Olaf Tans, Carla Zoethout and Jit Peters, entitled: *National Parliaments and European Democracy: A Bottom-up Approach to European Constitutionalism* (Groningen: Europa Law Publishing 2007). It takes the view that the political systems of the Member States are to be the prime source of inspiration to the process of supranational norms.

The second subproject, set up and carried out by Maastricht University, concerns the various accountability mechanisms in the relationship between

[1] European Commission, *European Governance: A White Paper*, COM (2001) 428 final, p. 10.

governments and parliaments in the EU Member States. It is a comparative analysis, aimed at uncovering general principles and ideas that could be helpful in designing or improving constitutional rules to be applied in the relationship between the EU institutions. The result is a volume edited by Luc Verhey, Hansko Broeksteeg and Ilse Van den Driessche entitled: *Political Accountability in Europe: Which Way Forward?* (Groningen: Europa Law Publishing 2008). The book concludes that the various concepts of ministerial accountability as they exist in the Member States, cannot easily be transplanted to the European Union level. However, looking at accountability issues from a more practice-based perspective, one can formulate some practical guidelines which could be applied both at the national and at the European level.

The third and last subproject, under the direction of Utrecht University, concerns the accountability of the civil service. It especially goes into the nature and the functioning of the civil service working under the responsibility of the European Commission. This project differs from the two other projects in the sense that it takes a primarily empirical rather than a legal approach. It includes drawing parallels between the European civil service and the functioning of the civil service at national levels. The publication is expected in 2009.

5 Reflecting on Political Accountability and European Integration

Based on the results of the SaRO research project, this collection contains a number of contributions by academic experts and practitioners the concept of political accountability in several national jurisdictions and in the European Union. Some contributors were involved in the project, while others have been asked to reflect on the research results or more generally on the concept of political accountability in the context of European integration.

The book is structured as follows. It starts with a discussion of the concept of executive accountability by *Dawn Oliver*, who explores the meaning and context of accountability mechanisms at an abstract level. Then, the results of the three subprojects are presented by the researchers in charge. Each presentation is followed by a discussion by on or two academic or professional experts. The first subproject, which dealt with the role of national parliaments in holding Europe's executives to account, is presented by *Jit Peters* and discussed by *Philipp Kiiver.* The second subproject covering the concept of political accountability mechanisms in Europe is presented by *Luc Verhey*, followed by commentaries from *Veith Medhe, Michael Shackleton* and *Jan Jacob van Dijk*. The third subproject, which involved an empirical study of civil service accountability, is presented by *Anchrit Wille* and discussed by *Thomas Christiansen* and *Walter van Gerven.*

The book concludes with several discussions on the future of executive accountability in the European context. *Deirdre Curtin* addresses the specific nature of the Council of Ministers as an executive institution linked to the legislative power at both the national level and the European level. *Bruno de Witte* then discusses executive accountability mechanisms as enshrined in the ill-fated Constitutional Treaty and in the Lisbon Treaty. Finally, *Paul Craig* demonstrates a three-step methodology for approaching executive accountability in the UK and in the EU, which looks at what executive functions are, what an executive institution is, and what the best way of securing executive accountability is.

The editors wish to thank the contributors to this book and all others who, in one way or another, have made the research project and the final conference possible.

Luc Verhey
Philipp Kiiver
Sandor Loeffen

Maastricht, February 2009

CHAPTER 2

Executive Accountability: A Key Concept

Dawn Oliver

In this paper I shall consider some of the ramifications of provisions for the accountability of executive bodies. Although this collection of essays is concerned with political accountability, my focus will include non-political mechanisms for executive accountability, since each mechanism needs to be seen in the wider context. We shall all have in mind the accountability of the European Commission, and to an extent of the Council and the European Council in what follows (see for instance Craig and Tomkins, 2006, chapter 11). But I shall approach the subject of executive accountability abstractly. I draw some of my examples from the position in the United Kingdom, but my points will, I hope, be of general application and thus transferable. I shall consider first, the broader context in which accountability mechanisms operate; then, the meanings of 'executive' and 'functions'; thirdly, the elements of the concept of accountability; and lastly, four particular kinds of accountability, according to the bodies or collections of people to whom executive bodies are accountable.

1 Accountability in Context: Good Governance

First let us put accountability in constitutional context. Accountability is an element in the requirements of good governance. This term is used as shorthand for a number of principles. It needs to be distinguished from 'governance', which is often used to refer to the use of networks or partnerships for the delivery of policy (see Harlow, 2002, pp. 178-186). Broadly good governance requires that government, including executive bodies, observe the following principles:

- openness and transparency;
- there should be in place appropriate provisions to maximise the effectiveness of government;
- public participation is to be encouraged;
- and, of course, there should be appropriate mechanisms of accountability, whether political, legal, public or auditing.

Further, constitutional arrangements should promote:

- legitimacy;
- trustworthiness, which implies encouraging trust and co-operation between state institutions;
- reliability;
- an absence of corruption;
- respect for human rights.

A range of techniques may be employed to give effect to good governance principles, some legal and some political or administrative. Our focus here is on the technique of accountability. But we need to bear in mind that there are additional techniques in play to promote good governance. Accountability is not the whole story.

Accountability, both within nation states and in the EU, may be viewed through the lens of evolutionary psychology and neuroscience (Ridley, 1996; Buss, 2007). These disciplines identify certain predispositions which are hard wired in the human brain. The contributions that these disciplines can make to the understanding of political processes are only now coming to be recognised. By way of illustration of the insights we can derive from these sciences, the European Union is a brilliant example of the use by the species *homo sapiens sapiens* of trade and exchange – a hard wired predisposition which is not shared by other animals – as a strategy for avoiding conflict between groups, here nations. Trade is a technique for promoting some of the essential and unique aspects of human social living and of avoiding or settling conflict between groups. It includes exchange of goods, services and the like, and – importantly – the exchanges that take place in the negotiation of relationships between individuals and groups. The EU, like all political organisations, functions on the basis of cooperation within and between organisations, of ongoing relationships of reciprocal altruism, and, where a party or organisation 'defects' or breaks the rules, ostracism and a strategies of tit for tat and punishment to bring the defector back into line. Thus accountability may be viewed as a way of securing that all parties to the EU project – the Member States and European Institutions – are honouring their obligations under it and thus avoiding escalating serious conflicts and ostracism.

2 The Executive

Having placed accountability in the context of good governance, we need to clarify what kinds of body are covered by the term 'executive bodies', the subject matter of this paper. They take many forms. They may be elected or appointed, political or politically neutral, experts or generalists. Political executives if elected have their own authority and legitimacy, and this will weigh in the scales when they are being held accountable: they may counter any criticisms made of them by their Parliaments and others to whom they are accountable by their own, possibly conflicting, claims to democratic legitimacy and authority.

Appointed, neutral executive bodies operate in a different dynamic. Such bodies include the European Commission, and, in the Member States, officials – civil servants – and independent agencies such as the Bank of England and the many agencies that have been set up in recent years under New Public Management theory. A point about these bodies is that they do not have their own democratic (i.e. electoral) legitimacy to weigh in the scales when criticised or held to account by others, particularly political bodies such as political executives or Parliaments. The authority and legitimacy of such neutral, independent bodies derives from their mandate, their line managers, if any, the very fact of their political neutrality, and their professional expertise. The clarity of the mandate, and the willingness of those holding them to account to use the mandate as the source of accountability criteria or standards will influence the way in which accountability mechanisms operate in relation to these appointed, neutral executive bodies.

And lastly, executive bodies may be experts or generalists. Those with relevant expertise may have legitimacy and generate trust which generalists lack. Civil servants are commonly not experts in the substantive areas with which they are concerned, and their legitimacy will derive from their political neutrality and administrative efficiency and belief in their bona fide commitment to the public interest – their altruism in evolutionary psychology terms.

Executive functions

Executive bodies' functions are varied, and different forms of accountability may be applicable according to the particular function under consideration. The functions may include: the formulation of policy, the making of subordinate legislation to implement such policy, the taking of legislative initiatives, participation in the legislative process, initiation of prosecutions and other judicial processes, and actual policy implementation and administration – which may require negotiation. At each stage 'political skills' may be required. While policy implementation and administration may be relatively technocratic, not calling for politically-driven accountability, policy formulation and legislative activities will attract both technocratic and politically based challenge.

Collaboration and participation in executive matters

A complicating factor in some organisations, notably the EU, is that there may be collaboration between executive bodies in these matters, with the result that responsibility and thus accountability may be shared, split or fragmented – or it may disappear in a fog of ambiguity. Collaboration may take place between bodies within and outside the accountability system, as where networks operate: collaboration between EU institutions and institutions in the Member States or between regulators in a number of Member States (for instance in relation to competition) are examples. Here the effectiveness of accountability arrangements, and their outcomes, will depend upon the mandates of the various bodies and the clarity of responsibility lines between them. But accountability can merge into or be swallowed up by partnership or participatory arrangements to which some kinds of accountability mechanism – public accountability, for instance – do not readily apply.

A danger in some forms of participatory democracy, or in shared, collective or collegial decision making, is that if things go wrong it may not be clear whose fault, if anyone's, the mistake was, and thus it may be difficult to impose accountability and to obtain redress or just satisfaction and thus catharsis and closure. In a system where there has been wide consultation and participation in decision making and the decision is later exposed to serious criticism, it will be open to the committee or other decision maker to say: 'Don't blame us. We consulted and this is what the public wanted us to do.' The fact that the public or a public wants a policy or a decision does not of course mean that it will turn out to be a wise or lawful or successful policy or decision. Normally decision-makers should accept that it is part of their job to take wise decisions and to exercise leadership, if necessary against the will of the public, and to accept responsibility in the sense of blame or credit for the outcomes.

3 The Concept of Accountability

Next we need to explore the very concept of accountability (see Oliver, 2003, chapter 3). We have already noted that it is but one element of good governance arrangements.

The point of accountability

Accountability may be said to entail being liable to be required to give an account or explanation of actions and, where appropriate, to suffer the consequences – for instance taking the blame (or credit) or undertaking to put matters right if it should appear that errors have been made (see generally Marshall, 1989; Woodhouse, 1997; Oliver and Drewry, 1996). Accountability mechanisms are the constitutional or systemic solution to the problem of fallibility around which the liberal-democratic tradition has been built up. No body and no party is infallible and no particular substantive policy can be assumed to be right. It is essential that the system and the processes – the rules of the game – that it entails, recognise these factors and provide safeguards against bad government and bad governance. Decision-makers must be obliged to justify their acts and not be allowed to rely on claims that their rightness is to be assumed. It must be permissible to advance alternative policies. There must in other words be contestability. We have moved from acceptance of authority as the basis of government and legitimacy as in feudal systems or where Divine Right is the basis of the right to rule. Instead, we require justification, a process by which the legitimacy of a ruling body and its policies are continually re-evaluated and renewed and checks are made on conformity to the objectives of the project in question. Legitimacy and trust are closely related. The knowledge on the part of decision makers that they will have to explain and justify their decisions and actions after the event (accountability is retrospective) ought to secure that those decisions and actions are properly and carefully considered before they are made. The procedures and mechanisms for making processes of accountability effective are thus central concerns of a liberal-democratic constitution – and I include the EU as a liberal democratic set of arrrangements.

Accountability furthers important objectives. It is supposed to promote openness, effectiveness and public participation and it is part of the system for safeguarding an uncorrupt system from corruption. It is central to the promotion of good governance. Bovens refers to this as a constitutional rationale for accountability: this is not a term the British would use. This is not just because we do not have a Constitution, but because 'constitutional' has a strong normative and substantive meaning in the UK. It is concerned with corruption, or course, but also with much broader issues such as protection of human rights, altruism, public service and so on.

Bovens (2006, 2007) also suggests that another rationale for accountability is democratic. Here it is British scepticism and fussiness about words and concepts that provokes a response. 'Democratic' is an extremely ambiguous word. Of course, to the extent that accountability is owed to the voting public and its representatives it may be said to be 'democratic'. But of course the collective views of the voting public are not necessarily right or wise. The executive is supposed to be wise and prudent, and not always to bend to democratic or popular pressures. That is what leadership is about. And that is what the duty to govern altruistically and disinterestedly in the public interest is also about. In the real world democracy is not about the people delegating power to their representatives. It is largely about government taking place with the consent or acquiescence of the people. Accountability, especially in the EU, is largely about ensuring that government or EU institutions act in the relevant public interest, with the consent of the people and their representatives on the Council.

Again, evolutionary psychology offers us insights here: governing institutions both in nation states and in the EU are supposed to operate to further the general public – or population's or citizens' interest. That is what public service (altruism in EP terms) is about in this context. This entails an assumption that there is 'a public', that the governed population or collection of citizens constitutes a group. There may of course be subgroups within that group. But if the population is not considered to be one group by the government, or does not consider itself to be a group – a demos if you like – then the governing body either loses authority or becomes authoritarian or has to resort to 'trade' of various kinds with the leaders of other 'publics'. This requires continual negotiation and renegotiation of disputes and relationships between groups, cooperation and reciprocity. Accountability arrangements should be designed both to avoid conflicts that cannot be resolved by negotiation and to foster cooperation and reciprocal relationships.

Certain kinds of accountability may undermine democracy or the constitution. Accountability of the executive in a one party, e.g. communist, state to the single, e.g. communist, party would not necessarily strike everyone as either democratic or 'constitutional' in a normative sense. An important point here is that accountability is not always a good thing. The trick is to achieve the appropriate web of accountability mechanisms, a topic we come to in due course.

Accountability and legitimacy

Accountability deficits may compromise legitimacy (see Bovens, 2006) and therefore undermine trust. The individual and collective responsibility of ministers in the UK to Parliament is a significant aspect of the legitimacy arrangements in the UK. However, accountability owed to an inappropriate body, one which is concerned to promote its own, rather than relevant public, interests will not increase legitimacy in the eyes of other groups and interests, or trust. Accountability of the Labour Government in the 1970s to the trade unions in fact undermined its legitimacy and was a factor in the rise to power of the Conservative government under Mrs Thatcher in 1979.

Accountability and responsibility, policy and operational matters

Accountability and responsibility are not the same, but the two words are often used interchangeably (see Birch, 1964). 'Responsibility' is a particularly ambiguous word. It can refer to a person's job: 'John is responsible for our publications' means that it is John's job to make sure our publications are produced. But it can also suggest that a person is prudent and wise: 'John is a very responsible person' does not mean that he has lots of jobs, but that he is conscientious, prudent and wise. And lastly 'responsible' may mean 'responsive' or 'accountable'. We need to bear these subtleties of meaning in mind when discussing accountability in what follows.

Recently attempts have been made in the UK to separate policy and operational decisions, and to allocate accountability separately to those responsible for each category. This has raised problems as to the 'job description' of those (ministers in the case of the UK) who are responsible for policy, and whether their responsibility extends to the proper resourcing of operational matters and oversight of them, including a duty to reorganise activities of an operational kind that are supposed to be giving effect to policies. The upshot of this has been acceptance on the part of ministers that they do have such responsibilities (jobs) and are accountable if they do not perform them properly (Oliver, 2003, pp. 225-228). The issue illustrates the difficulties and possible lacunae in accountability where jobs are shared between politicians and others and a range of accountability mechanisms apply.

Accountability and trust

Next, accountability and trust. Trust is valuable social capital in any community (Fukuyama, 1995; Ridley, 1996, chapter 13; O'Neill, 2002): it affects the form of economic development – private enterprise, an important aspect of the European project. Its absence may mean that economic development takes place in the form of public ownership of industry rather than private enterprise – China is an example. As humans we are uniquely equipped with the capacity to trust (Ridley, 1996) but whether that capacity flourishes will depend upon the environment and culture in which individuals operate. In my view this capacity for trust and its nurturing are fundamental, even foundational, to the proper operation of democracy and good government.

However, what has all this to do with accountability? Inappropriate accountability can undermine the level of trust in society, inhibit economic development and lead to over-bureaucratisation. O'Neill discusses this in her Reith lectures,

2002. It could even increase untrustworthy behaviour. O'Neill (2002) suggests that there seems to be no evidence that public trust is reviving as a result of the increase in regulation and accountability in the system, and she asks whether continuing expressions of mistrust suggest that we are imposing the wrong sort of accountability. She points out that some accountability mechanisms conflict with others and are incoherent and that this invites compromises and evasions and undermines both professional judgment and institutional autonomy. The pursuit of ever more perfect accountability provides us with more information, more comparisons, more complaints systems, but it also builds a culture of suspicion and low morale, and may ultimately lead to professional cynicism – and then we would have grounds for public mistrust. O'Neill suggests that what is needed is 'intelligent accountability', with more attention paid to good governance as a whole rather than over-concentration on accountability. Institutions need to be allowed some margin for self-governance within a framework of financial and other *reporting*. 'Serious and effective accountability ... needs to concentrate on good governance, on obligations to tell the truth and needs to seek intelligent accountability. If we want a culture of public service, professionals and public servants must in the end be free to serve the public rather than their paymasters'. An emphasis on reporting rather than auditing (except for financial propriety) could indeed counteract the distorting effects of targets, performance indicators and the like.

Criteria or standards for imposing accountability

As we shall see accountability comes in many shapes and sizes. An issue with each accountability mechanism is – by what criteria or standards will the accountor be held to account? Do these standards promote or undermine the objectives of the institution – in our case the EU. In some forms of accountability – judicial review, the Ombudsmen – the criteria are set out in legal sources – Acts of Parliament or case law. In others they are found in soft-law documents such as benchmarks, Citizen's Charters, performance indicators, public service agreements, framework documents, the Seven Principles of Public Life and the like. They may be part of the 'law and custom of Parliament' or similar, largely cultural rather than legal sources. We ought to be able to assume, in democracies, that all of these standards do indeed promote the institution's collective objective. In yet other forms of accountability – particularly where the 'accountees' are politicians, the criteria will be fluid, unarticulated or non existent – and they may not promote the collective objectives of the institutions. They may depend upon public opinion, political opportunism or sectional self-interest.

The tightness of criteria for accountability is of importance both for the effectiveness of accountability after the event, and also for improving initial decision making. Uncertainty about accountability standards may lead risk-averse accountors to take particular care not to displease potential accountees – a widespread experience in former communist countries: this can lead to excessive bureaucracy, refusal to take responsibility and ultimately paralysis – the experience in many countries in the Soviet Union.

Rewards, redress or punishment

We should avoid taking too negative a view of accountability: it can be a mechanism for praise and reward, including intangible rewards such as enhanced status and trust. But there must also be provision for matters to be put right when things have gone wrong – for redress – or for punishment of some kind, including ostracism and shaming: one must never neglect the non-legal processes at work in communities. A sense of obligation to put things right only arises if a position has been reached where either the decision-maker accepts that something went wrong, or the accountee makes a finding to that effect. There may well be difficulties in convincing the accountor of their redress obligation in the absence of the sword of Damocles – an authoritative finding to that effect by the accountee. Even where the accountor has given explanation and justification, the facts may remain in dispute or the persuasiveness of the explanation and justification may be contested by the accountee – as was the case in the aftermath of the Scott Report on Arms to Iraq in 1995 (Tomkins, 1998). Where the accountee does reach a view on the matter, the effectiveness of that finding will depend upon the pressure that the accountee can bring to bear on the accountor to make redress. If *legal* accountability is in issue, then the redress – by court order – will be coercively enforceable. But in other forms of accountability the enforceability of redress will vary. It may depend upon who, if anyone, has the authority to impose redress, for instance to dismiss an official found to be at fault.

Redress may be secured informally, for instance via cultural expectations – as is commonly the case where the UK Parliamentary Ombudsman makes critical findings, particularly if the parliamentary committee to which she reports – the Public Administration Select Committee – supports her. Here again evolutionary psychology provides helpful insights. Cultural expectations can be effective in securing redress where a sense of common identity and community between the decision maker and the accountee is present. If that common identity or sense of community does not exist, then decision-makers will not find mere cultural or social pressures persuasive and may get away with ignoring them. This in turn will undermine the authority of the accountee – and enhance the status of the accountor. More formal pressures may be required, for instance legal ones, in such circumstances.

The duty to give redress may be discharged in various ways, depending upon the expectations and culture of the organisations involved. Redress may involve acceptance of blame and an apology from the decision maker: in some situations this will satisfy the critics. Or it may require the payment of *ex gratia* or legally ordered compensation to 'victims' of a decision. In some situations what is expected will be reversal of the decision or policy under challenge, or undertakings to make sure that bureaucratic errors do not recur. This may involve increasing the resources available to the body in question to enable it to function better, or reorganising the system. Ultimately, voluntary resignation or imposed dismissal may be the only ways in which accountees can be satisfied – and closure and catharsis achieved.

Dismissal as a sanction will depend upon who has the power of dismissal. In the UK, for instance, only the Prime Minister may dismiss a minister. The House of Commons may, theoretically, pass a vote of no confidence in a minister and even reduce his salary. But this never happens because a Minister in that position will have resigned or been removed by the Prime Minister before then. The culture is powerful here because ministers all belong to Parliament and that body itself has a set of expectations as to how ministers should respond to criticism.

Accountability and responsiveness

Accountability summons up an image of criticism of a body that is expected to respond in some way. As we have noted it is often assumed that the response to criticism will be an offer of redress. However, the willingness of the accountee to respond, or the style of response, will depend on a number of factors. First, the remoteness or proximity of the critic to the accountee. Generally if the critic is remote from the accountee there will be only weak pressure on the latter to respond positively to the criticism. Response will also be affected by the authority of the critic. The legitimacy and cogency of the criticism will affect the response of the accountee. For instance, the reports of the UK House of Lords on European issues are generally highly regarded. This is a function of the authority of the members of the European Union Committee and its subcommittees, and linked to that the cogency of their arguments. But other chambers of other parliaments of Member States, all of which lack proximity to the executive bodies of the EU, have relatively weak authority and produce, as I understand it, reports of relatively weak cogency. The reports of such bodies are unlikely to elicit positive responses from EU institutions.

Responsibility and leadership

Responsibility and leadership are crucial elements in an accountability system. Acceptance of the importance of accountability and participatory democracy should not undermine the equal if not greater importance of responsibility in the system. We have already noted that 'responsibility' has many meanings. It includes the ideas (i) that a person has a job to do, (ii) that they should be prudent, and (iii) that they are answerable or accountable for how they do their job. It means that there should be an identifiable person or body with the job of making decisions. That body should be accountable for those decisions, and take the credit or blame if they turn out to have been wrong. The UK tradition places a high priority on prudent decision-making, more so than on responsive decision making or accountability (Birch, 1964).

Collective responsibility

Collective responsibility of a body (e.g. the British government) or a commission or council may require that any disagreements between the members should not be revealed and that all members of the body should support the decision and take the blame for it if it turns out to have been wrong. Collective responsibility is supposed to facilitate frank discussion before a decision is made so that the implications, positive and negative, can be aired without fear of unfair or partisan criticism from outside. This is generally conducive to wise decision making. But it can serve to shield those who successfully advocated the decision from criticism outside the collective body if that decision turns out to have been unwise: collective responsibility can undermine accountability. On the other hand if collective responsibility also involves, as in the UK, an obligation on the whole of the executive to resign in case of loss of confidence, it is a powerful form of accountability. Again, this virtually never happens. When it does this is normally, in the UK at least, because of a loss of parliamentary majority as a result of by-elections or floor-crossings, or collapse of a coalition or pact. The imperative here is that in a parliamentary system the government cannot function if it does not have a parliamentary majority. That imperative does not necessarily exist where an executive body is not dependant upon a political majority, as in EU institutions.

Summary

Ultimately in the liberal-democratic tradition it is for their stewardship of the relevant regional, national or Europe-wide public interest that executive bodies are in practice most commonly accountable, and by this criterion that they are judged. So in considering questions such as: 'to whom is a minister/ commission/ council etc to be accountable?' 'by what standards is an official to be held accountable?' and 'by what mechanism is accountability to be imposed?' it is important not to lose sight of the fact that the public interest is the ultimate legitimating justification for executive bodies, and accountability should promote this. However, there is an added complication in Europe, which does not exist in Member States: what is 'the public' whose interests the executive is supposed to promote? For the Commission the public is theoretically the whole of the EU: yet individual Commissioners my be under pressure to favour their own state's interests; for the Parliament it is the people of Europe: but their own party's interests may slant the approach of each MEP; and for the members of the Council it is their own countries. For the peoples, it is probably their own people/nation. There is in other words a web of possibly conflicting accountability pressures – what Bovens (2007) calls 'a more diversified and pluralistic set of accountability mechanisms' – and a web of possibly inconsistent, contradictory standards for accountability in the European arrangements, which is more complex than in the Member States – though federal states such a Germany, where the upper House represents the members of the federation may also produce some such webs.

So much for the concept of accountability. It is helpful in analysing executive accountability to distinguish four classes of body to whom accountability is owed – accountees: these are politicians, the public, the courts, and a range of 'auditors' – the term has a special meaning in this context. We shall consider them in turn.

4 Accountability to Elected Politicians

First, accountability to elected politicians. In parliamentary systems the executive will be accountable to the Parliament, the Prime Minister and the Cabinet; in the European context the parallels would be the Commission's accountability to the European Parliament and Council. Here a note about terminology may be helpful. It is sometimes suggested that the European Parliament 'controls' the Commission, or more generally that executive bodies are or should be subject to such 'control'. In English in this context 'control' would imply direction, command or regulation in advance of a decision being made. That is not what accountability means. We shall be concerned here rather with scrutiny and checking of executive decisions and actions, after the event, which is what 'contrôler' (French) and 'controllare' (Italian) mean.

The point about political accountability is that it exposes the bodies to politically-motivated scrutiny, and to open censure through elected institutions. Given that the European Commission is supposed at once to be neutral and to promote the interests of the whole EU, a question arises as to the appropriateness of exposing it to politically partisan forms of accountability, whether to the Parliament which represents the people of Europe, or the Council which represents the interests of the Member States or indeed to the parliaments of Member States. I do not feel able to resolve this question, save to note that the Commission is also accountable to the Court of Auditors and the ECJ, it operates within a web of accountability and the cumulative effect of this accountability web ought not to be to undermine the overall mission of the Commission.

Political accountability standards

We have already noted that the standards by which a body is judged in political accountability tend to be more fluid than the standards imposed by, for instance, accountability to the courts or to auditors of various kinds: this is both because there may not be a clear 'job description' or 'mission' to which the official or accountable person can be held by politicians, and partly because politicians tend not to consider themselves limited by such matters in the way in which they impose accountability. In political accountability an official may be judged according to whether, for instance, their actions have met with public approval or criticism, almost regardless of what they set out to do, or whether they have succeeded in meeting objectives (which is often difficult to assess), such as increasing prosperity or improving public health.

In parliamentary systems there may be provisions to protect civil servants and officials from being exposed to accountability or at least to politically motivated criticism, in order to preserve the tradition of a permanent, professional, non partisan civil service. In the UK for instance, though civil servants may appear before parliamentary select committees to be questioned, they answer questions on behalf of and at the direction of their minister. They are not entitled to make their own independent comments about government policy. Nowadays they are increasingly exposed to personal criticism in these committees, but this is a departure from the earlier strict rules about anonymity. The senior official in a government department or agency is the accounting officer for the department or agency and in that capacity is directly and personally accountable to Parliament for their use of public money. But the financial accountability criteria are relatively precise and defined.

Procedures

The procedures for imposing political accountability are also often less formal than those for legal accountability (in litigation strict rules of procedure have to be followed) or in audit (the ombudsmen, the National Audit Office and the Audit Commission carry out their investigations with some formality – see below). In parliamentary systems ministers are themselves members of the body to which they are accountable – Parliament – and their supporters are likely to be in the majority in Parliament, which weakens accountability. This is obviously not the case in Europe. We should also note that the sanctions where the machinery of political accountability imposes a duty to make amends are not generally legally coercive but political: a minister's duty to undertake to put things right or to resign is a matter of convention rather than law.

Effectiveness

Political accountability is not always as effective as it should be. For instance, parliamentarians often lack forensic skills and so are not able to extract the information they need in order to hold executive bodies to account. Or they may be influenced by ulterior political considerations to be critical or supportive of executive bodies. It matters therefore that there are other accountability mechanisms, in other words an accountability web.

Appropriateness

Political accountability may be inappropriate for some executive bodies or functions, especially autonomous ones like, in the UK, the Bank of England. In many parliamentary systems autonomous or quasi autonomous bodies are established in recognition of the fact that certain activities of an executive nature should not be directly subject to political accountability. Examples from the UK include the Bank of England, the Higher Education Funding Councils which distribute public money to universities, and the many regulators of utilities, financial services and other areas of the economy. There are, as we shall see, a range of forms of accountability and within each form a variety of particular mechanisms; this is the moment at which to observe that an important aspect of good governance arrangements is securing that the most appropriate forms or combination of forms, of accountability are applied to public bodies.

5 Accountability to the Public or Sections of the Public

'At large' accountability

In discussing public accountability we must remember that we are not concerned with whether the mechanism is public in the sense of being open (cf. Bovens, 2007), but with accountability *to* the general public or *to* interested sections of the public including professional and other peers. This is sometimes called social or horizontal accountability (Bovens, 2007) because it involves direct unmediated accountability lines between the accountor and public or a section of it. Pressure and responses from the public can be powerful factors in extracting explanations and justifications from executive bodies and leading to redress of various kinds.

In parliamentary and other democratic systems Ministers, Members of Parliament, and some public officials are in practice under obligations to explain and justify their actions to the public. The public 'judgment' will be very much 'at large'. Commonly there are no set criteria or standards against which the public or sections of it criticise and reach conclusions about executive's decisions and actions. In some countries patronage, corruption, inefficiency and waste of public money are less unacceptable than in others, for instance. Officials may find themselves obliged through pressures of criticism and embarrassment to make amends where errors have been made. This can be an effective mechanism in liberal democratic states where officials feel committed to the public so that the culture of accountability and responsiveness is strong. Whether these mechanisms are so effective in relation to the EU may be doubted. If the Commission is considered remote by ordinary people and sections of the population of Europe, and if the Commission itself considers those people to be remote, then public accountability without political support is unlikely to be effective.

On the other hand where accountability is owed to professional peers there are likely to be shared professional values and standards and a culture which provides and promotes those standards.But it is not unknown for professionals to close ranks to protect their own members against criticism from outside.

The 'publics' to whom accountability is owed

In any event, 'the public' is not monolithic. There are different publics with different needs and wishes in the nations and regions of Europe. Indeed, 'the public' in relation to Europe has special dimensions in that it includes the various peoples of Europe, and the Parliaments of Member States. Executive bodies in Europe are exposed to criticism from within Member States, and pressures to take into account the particular needs of their peoples or sections of them.

'The public' is also divisible in other ways, for instance in relation to different categories of consumer of public services – acutely and chronically ill patients, sufferers from different ailments, for instance – or a range of interest groups. These interests may not always have effective 'voices' at European level through which their interests may be made known and responded to.

Effectiveness

The effectiveness of accountability to the public or publics depends on the availability of information – openness. An ill-informed public cannot hold executive bodies to account effectively for their care of the public interest. Hence the freedom of the media to report on matters of public interest, and public rights of access to official information and freedom of speech are crucial to the effectiveness of this form of accountability.

Appropriateness

As with political accountability, public accountability is not always appropriate. Some matters must be kept confidential and therefore immune from public scrutiny (certain matters to do with national security, the detection and prevention of crime, sensitive foreign relations). The design of accountability mechanisms should be such as to secure that public accountability does not promote sectional interests at the expense of the general public interest. The use of social partners and cross-sectoral social partners negotiating framework agreements seems to me to pose a danger of subordinating general public interests to sectoral interests.

6 Accountability to Courts and Tribunals

The rule of law

Thirdly, legal accountability, normally accountability to courts and tribunals. The legal accountability of executive bodies is an important aspect of the rule of law. The duty to obey the law, enforceable by action in courts and tribunals at the instigation of those affected by the actions of public bodies, imposes an obligation on a public body to explain and justify its actions against legal criteria and to make amends if found to have transgressed.

An important respect in which legal accountability differs from other forms is that the remedies and sanctions are coercive: generally public bodies can be compelled by the courts to perform their legal duties and to refrain from unlawful acts.

Appropriateness

As with political and public accountability, accountability to the courts is not always the appropriate form. Pursuing actions against executive bodies in the courts is expensive and time-consuming; often alternative methods of resolving disputes will be more appropriate, for instance, via an ombudsman. There are problems over whether judges are competent to decide on the legality of executive action and whether political or administrative accountability (see below) would therefore be more appropriate. Much will depend on the clarity of the law: tax, financial services and social security law are elaborated in considerable detail. Judicial review is more fluid. Judges themselves may be conscious of this. In the UK judges regard certain matters as not 'justiciable' (*Council of Civil Service Unions v. Minister for the Civil Service* [1985] AC 374), for example disputes about national security, diplomatic matters, and foreign affairs. In such matters the courts are usually willing to defer to executive bodies and give them a margin of discretion when making politically charged decisions.

7 Accountability to Auditors, Inspectors and Administrative Bodies

Fourthly, there is audit and, linked with it, inspection and administrative accountability. These mechanisms may be applied both within and between governmental agencies and by independent external bodies.

Professional, independent accountees

Until recently audit has been connected with the function of professional examination of financial accounts, and auditors have been non-political experts in accounting – and counting. Dubnick (2002) suggests, interestingly, that this derives from the reign of William the Conqueror in England, the Domesday book being a famous example (see Bovens, 2006). In the UK the Treasury, the most powerful government department, audits expenditure by government departments and others in receipt of money from the Exchequer. The National Audit Office, headed by the Comptroller and Auditor General, is responsible for the audit of most government expenditure. The C & AG is an officer of Parliament, independent from government. He and his office report to the Public Accounts Committee of the House of Commons, which may in turn call the accounting officers of government departments before it to deal with concerns about accounts. This is taken very seriously both by the executive and by Parliament. Political accountability and audit come together in this field. The British government accepts that: 'An effective system of accountability of the Executive to Parliament, backed up by rigorous processes of audit, reporting and scrutiny, is fundamental to the proper operation of a Parliamentary democracy.' (Cm 5456, 2002; see also *Holding to Account* (the Sharman Report), 2001). I assume that similar systems operate in other Member States.

Non-financial audit

The term audit and the techniques associated with it have come to be used in relation to non-financial matters. Environmental audits involve assessing the impact of development on the environment; teaching quality audits involve examining the procedures for assessing the quality of teaching; and there are 'value for money' audits, intellectual property audits, regulatory impact audits, stress audits, and so on. There has in effect been an audit explosion (Power, 1994, 1999). Audit and inspection rely heavily on the formulation of relatively concrete standards against which performance can be measured. These criteria may be set out in statute, as is the case with audit under the National Audit Act 1983, or, more commonly, in 'soft law' form, such as performance indicators or Public Service Agreements.

In the context of this discussion of the kind of body to whom a person is accountable, 'auditor' and 'inspector' are useful terms to denote a range of non-political, expert public bodies, not limited in their operations to financial auditing and accounting. These bodies are concerned for the most part with non-political – i.e. non-party and non-partisan – matters such as maladministration leading to injustice, efficiency, effectiveness, value for money, and meeting targets.

It is only in the last twenty years or so that attention has focussed on these mechanisms of accountability. This form of audit has been quite developed in Sweden, for instance, for many years – and it is in some respects a substitute for political accountability (Richardson, 1982).

External audit

It is helpful to distinguish here between external and internal audit and inspection mechanisms. The *external* auditing relationships between public bodies involve auditing by bodies independent of the accountor: in the UK the independent bodies include the Comptroller and Auditor General, the National Audit Office, the Parliamentary Ombudsman, the Audit Commission. These external auditors have statutory coercive powers enabling them to gain access to documents and information about the matters under investigation. But the sanctions in this form of accountability are not generally legally coercive: the recommendations of the Parliamentary Ombudsman are advisory only. The Comptroller and Auditor General and the National Audit Office, in their reports on value for money, cannot impose legal sanctions. But they are taken very seriously by government departments. The principal weapons of these agencies are publicity and embarrassment, so there are links here with public and political accountability. These are often backed up by political pressures. The UK House of Commons Select Committee for Public Administration can apply pressure on ministers to comply with the Ombudsman's recommendations, and in practice this is usually effective. The Public Accounts Committee also has strong influence in securing that notice is taken of the reports of the National Audit Office. The proximity between the actors in these arrangements means that the culture of responsiveness is strong. These are examples of what Bovens (2006, 2007) calls diagonal accountability – the real line is from the auditor to the government, but it passes via a parliamentary committee.

Internal audit

The *internal* audit and inspection mechanisms – for instance the British Treasury's imposition of accountability on other Whitehall departments – may be viewed as forms of self-regulation. This kind of operation may be conceptualised nowadays as 'regulation inside government', to borrow the title of one of the leading UK monographs on the subject (see Hood, Scott et al., 1999. See also Daintith and Page, 1999). These relationships have been mapped and analysed by Daintith and Page, 1999. The accountees operating these mechanisms are for the most part non-political and professionally qualified, and they are concerned with particular and closely defined aspects of government. As Hood, Scott et al. put it, they are 'waste-watchers, quality police, and sleaze-busters'. But this form of internal control can become inflated and damaging to effectiveness. In the UK the Public Administration Select Committee found in 2001 that the Treasury had increased its influence over the affairs of spending departments to an unacceptable extent. Witnesses suggested that the interventionism of the Treasury in other departments was undermining both the Treasury's own effectiveness in its core work, and the effectiveness of departments. The Committee recommended, inter alia, that the Treasury's own targets, which it used to hold spending departments to account, should be externally validated, that the Treasury's influence in government should be decreased and that the Treasury itself should be accountable to the House of Commons' departmental select committees. I assume that similar problems of inflated internal self-regulation are liable to develop in any complex organisation.

Problems

Audit and inspection have, then, become fashionable forms of accountability, but they have a number of disadvantages:

- Imposing an audit or inspection regime on activity implies a lack of trust in the organisation or its members: lack of trust can generate untrustworthiness or demotivating loss of commitment to the activity (see Power, 1999, chapter 6; O'Neill, 2002);
- Audit can best measure quantities, not quality (Oliver and Drewry, 1996).
- Audit imposes considerable costs on those being audited;
- The criteria by which audit takes place can be difficult to define;
- Audit and inspection can have unintended adverse consequences;
- The auditors and inspectors themselves and their processes need to be open to audit and inspection.

What we can draw from this is not that audit or inspection are bad things, but that, as with other forms of accountability, proportionality in the sense of avoiding unnecessarily burdensome requirements is an important consideration in the design of accountability mechanisms (Power, 1999).

8 The Accountability of Accountees

The question may arise 'quis custodiet ipsos custodes'? Given the power that accountees possess, and the fact that we cannot assume that any accountee is necessarily exercising that power for proper purposes – in the public interest and altruistically – their own accountability is an issue. Politicians have to face the electorate from time to time, and they have to answer to press and public concerns from day to day. They are also accountable for their conduct to their own organisations – in the UK each member is accountable to his or her own House for conduct: misleading the House is about the worst offence known to politicians. Thus self-regulation is part of the web.

The public itself operates in a web of interrelated organisations of civil society – the political parties, the churches, trade unions and industrial bodies, sporting bodies, learned societies, universities, the professions and so on. Each of these bodies has rules which they will enforce within the membership. They all play a part in holding one another to account, for instance via press criticism, withholding cooperation, resolving disputes, negotiating for collaboration and so on.

Judges are accountable up the judicial hierarchy, and in the case of issues to do with European law and the European Convention on Human Rights, to the courts attached to those arrangements. And in the UK it is open to Parliament, theoretically at least, to overturn a decision of the courts by passing new legislation.

And auditors, inspectors and other administrative agencies are generally formally accountable to Parliament and to particular complainants, and informally to the public.

9 Webs of Accountability

Often accountability is imposed in more than one form and is directed to several bodies – politicians, the public, the courts and auditors and inspectors of various kinds.

Problems

But '[T]oo much accountability can be as problematic as too little. Certain organisations operate in a dense web of accountability demands which undermine its capacity to fulfil primary objectives' (Flinders, Richards and Smith evidence to the House of Commons Select Committee on Public Administration, quoted in Sixth Report of the Select Committee on Public Administration, HC 209, 1998-99, *Quangos*, at para. 102). To take an example close to the author's experience, the upward accountability of universities to the Higher Education Funding Councils is imposed through the quinquennial research assessment exercises, the periodic teaching quality assessments, and auditing of internal procedures. The processes involve peer review which should protect universities from political interference. But the processes are bureaucratic, and they impose substantial costs in terms of staff time and resources on the universities which might be better spent on teaching and research.

Another problem is that a body or an executive function may, despite the existence of elaborate webs of accountability, fall through a gap: the separation policy from operational matters would create such a gap. The European Council is an example of such a body since it is not accountable to the European Parliament, the Commission or institutions in the Member States (Van Gerven, 2005; Bovens, 2007): it is in some respects a corporate version of a medieval monarch.

Achieving a balance

Accountability mechanisms also have to be balanced so as to promote the overall objectives of the enterprise. Accountability processes can have unintended consequences, particularly where different objectives contradict one another or where the targets or criteria for accountability have been ill-thought out and contain perverse incentives. A crude example is provided by the bus driver whose performance was assessed according to the punctuality of his arrival at the terminus at the end of the route. Asked why he had driven past a queue of passengers at a bus stop, his reply was that he would have arrived late at the terminus if he had stopped to pick them up. To return to the universities, the research and teaching quality assessment exercises introduce incentives in the system in favour of universities concentrating resources on research, which is rewarded by the HEFCE, and diverting energies away from teaching, where there are no special rewards for high quality (see also Committee for Public Accounts 46th Report *Inappropriate Adjustments to NHS Waiting Lists*, HC 517, 2001-2002, and discussion in chapter 12).

10 Some Conclusions

Overall accountability arrangements should be designed to promote relevant, identified general public interests. Executive bodies should be compelled to justify their actions in those terms or in other constitutionally acceptable terms (justice, humanity, equity). The matter is made particularly complex at European level, more so than within Member States, because of the range of 'publics' whose interests the actors in the executive accountability web are supposed to promote or safeguard, and the range of publics to whom they are accountable.

The question, to whom is accountability owed? is often crucial to the good working of a system, as are the criteria against which a person's conduct is measured, and whether those criteria have been reduced to writing in legislation or a code, and the design of the mechanisms of accountability. Choices have to be made about the balance between the different forms of accountability – whether legal accountability is to be preferred to political accountability, or whether a number of forms of accountability can operate in parallel. But there are many ways in which accountability can go wrong, and finding the right mechanisms of accountability and the right balance between overlapping mechanisms and 'webs' for each particular accountor and function is a subtle and complex business.

References

Birch, A. H. *Representative and Responsible Government,* George, Allen and Unwin, 1964.

Bovens, M. 'Analysing and assessing public accountability: A conceptual framework' European Governance Papers (EUROGOV) No. C-06-01, 2006, http://www.connex-network.org/eurogov/pdf/egp-connex-C-06-01.pdf.

Bovens, M. 'New forms of accountability and EU-Governance' 5 *Comparative European Politics,* 2007, 104-120.

Buss, D.M. *Evolutionary Psychology. The New Science of the Mind,* Pearson, 2007.

Craig, P. P. and Tomkins, A. *The Executive and Public Law,* OUP, 2006.

Craig, P.P. 'The locus and accountability of the Executive in the EU' in Craig, P. P. and Tomkins, A. *The Executive and Public Law,* OUP, 2006.

Dubnick, M.J. 'Seeking salvation for accountability'. Paper presented at the annual meeting of the American Political Science Association, Boston 2002. Cited in Bovens, 2006.

Daintith, T.C. and Page, A. *The Executive in the Constitution,* OUP, 1999.

Fukuyama, F. *Trust: The Social Virtues and the Creation of Prosperity,* Hamish Hamilton, 1995.

Harlow, C. *Accountability in the European Union,* OUP, 2002.

Hood, C., Scott, C. et al, *Regulation inside Government. Waste-Watchers, Quality Police and Sleaze*-Busters, OUP, 1999.

Marshall, G. *Ministerial Responsibility,* OUP, 1989.

O'Neill, O. *A Question of Trust,* CUP, 2002.

Oliver, D. and Drewry, G. *Public Service Reforms. Issues of Accountability and Public Law,* Pinter, 1996.

Oliver, D. *Constitutional Reform in the United Kingdom,* OUP, 2003.

Power, M. *The Audit Explosion,* Demos, 1994.

Power, M. *The Audit Society. Rituals of Verification,* OUP. 1999.

Richardson, J. J. 'Programme evaluation in Britain and Sweden' 35 *Parliamentary Affairs,* 160-80, 1982.

Ridley, M. *The Origins of Virtue,* 1996.

Tomkins, A. *The Constitution after Scott,* 1998.

Van Gerven, W. *The European Union:A Polity of States and Peoples.* Hart Publishing, 2005.

Woodhouse, D. *In Pursuit of Good Administration,* Clarendon Press, 1997.

CHAPTER 3

The Role of National Parliaments

Checks and Balances between the EU and the Member States

Jit Peters

1 Introduction

In my contribution, I will ask myself the question if the powers given to the national parliaments by the Lisbon Treaty in controlling the powers of the Union are sufficient as a countervailing power against the ever-expanding competences of the Union.

Article 5 of the consolidated draft Union Treaty as amended by the Treaty of Lisbon reads as follows:

1. The limits of Union competences are governed by the principle of conferral. The use of Union competences is governed by the principles of subsidiarity and proportionality.

2. Under the principle of conferral, the Union shall act only within the limits of the competences conferred upon it by the Member States in the Treaties to attain the objectives set out therein. Competences not conferred upon the Union in the treaties remain with the Member States.

So far, this attribution principle and the subsidiarity principle has had a very limited meaning in protecting the national competences. The European Court of Justice has always given a broad interpretation of the competences of the EU.[1] It is a popular misunderstanding that European citizens' lack of interest in the European Union has to do with the lack of powers of the European Parliament. These powers have been constantly strengthened over the years, but that did not enhance the interest of the voters in European affairs. Even the granting of European citizenship and the introduction of the euro did not get the voters interested, as the low turnout at the elections of members of the European Parliament in The Netherlands on June 2004 (less than 45 percent) attests. These elections even saw the rise of anti-European parties in several member-states, like the Independence party (UKIP) in the United Kingdom. Besides, these elections were more about national issues and the confidence in national governments than they were about European issues.

The lack of interest partly has to do with the lack of transparency in decision-making. The existing legislative procedures are difficult to explain to the average law student, let alone to the ordinary citizen.[2] That the decision making process at the European level is conceived to be technical and bureaucratic is also part of the problem. This doesn't help to catch the attention of the mass media, which in its turn doesn't help to get the citizens involved.

The fact is that a citizen of Europe for the moment does not feel himself to be a European citizen, but one of France or Germany, or Paris or Hamburg. A reason for this is, of course, the familiarity of national or local democratic procedures. The European citizen knows the national or local politicians and at times has at least the impression that he can influence decisions made by "his" politi-

1 Prof. Dr. L. Hancher and Dr. A. van den Brink, 'Versterken van de legitimiteit van de EU in Nederland', *NJB* 2007, p. 2808.

2 Jit Peters, 'National Parliaments and Subsidiarity: Think Twice', *European Constitutional Law Review*, 1: p. 68-72, 2005.

cians. There is also a strong need for decentralisation as a consequence of the unavoidable globalisation and the feeling of a decrease of democratic influence. The same phenomena play their part in the European Union. The principle of subsidiarity, which requires that decisions should be taken at the lowest possible level, has been introduced to counter the expansion of (the use) of powers of the European Union. The principle of subsidiarity thus might help support the citizens' want for decision making on a more decentralized level. As such, subsidiarity is necessary for the Union's democratic legitimacy. It is also logical to entrust to national parliaments the role of watchdog when it comes to the application of this principle, as the Protocol on the application of the principles of subsidiarity and proportionality, attached of the Lisbon Treaty, does. Yet how difficult it is, even for the national parliaments, to play their role as watchdog will be made clear in this contribution.

2 The Ever-Expanding Competences of the Union

There is a natural tendency to continually expand the powers and competences of the Union, at the costs of the Member States' powers. This is not the consequence of a conspiracy of the institutions of the Union, or a group of people within the Union, but the natural tendency of all the institutions of the Union; and not of the Union alone. The attitude of the Member States also contributes to this trend.

The EU Commission exists nowadays of 27 members. All these members have interesting tasks and territories to wield them on. Commissioner Markos Kyprianou is not only responsible for health but also for the welfare of animals. Commissioner Viviane Reding, responsible for Information Policy and media, is also expected to contribute to the improvement of health. Commissioner Figel is not only responsible for education and culture but also for youth. These seem to me to be ever-expanding territories. If the Commissioners would like to make an impact, and let the people in their home state know that they are in charge, they should initiate new proposals that are going to challenge at least the principle of subsidiarity and proportionality.

With the European Parliament, it is quite the same. Generally speaking, most parliamentarians are believers in Europe. They can only show themselves to the electorate by becoming active in policy matters of the EU. Normally that is not characterized by stressing restraint on the policy proposals of the Commission. The EP is divided in 22 permanent committees resembling the portfolios of the commissioners. For example, the Committee on Culture and education is amongst others responsible for youth policy and the development of sports and leisure policy. This seems to me to be an ever-expanding territory for active parliamentarians.

To give just one example of the activities of members of the EP, one may think about the protection of people like Ayaan Hirsi Ali. A petition asking the

EU to protect Ayaan in the name of freedom of speech was signed by a hundred EU parliamentarians and put forward by four socialist members of the EP. Clearly a very sympathetic gesture, but so far the protection of threatened people was clearly thought of as belonging to the competence of national states and not of the EU.

The Council is also not the body to protect the national competences in relation to the EU. Although the Council exists out of ministers who are responsible or accountable to their national parliaments for their behaviour in the Council, the Council seldom plays the role of a brake on the powers of the EU. There is a natural tendency to compromise on policy matters and to bring the good news of new proposals that have been agreed upon, instead of boasting upon a negative attitude of frustrating new proposals. Ministers tend to be proud of positive results gained through compromises. This tendency is strengthened by the way the Council meets in separate sector councils. Sectional interests tend to be dominant during those meetings and overshadowing questions of competences. Nationally the coordination of EU policy affairs also tends to be dominated by sectional interests, at least in The Netherlands.[3] It is my personal experience, in five years as high civil servant attending the Council on environmental affairs, that the issue of subsidiarity or proportionality was never raised in the meeting of the Council, although sometimes there might have been reasons to do so.

The same is true of the Council working groups. The civil servants representing their national governments in the working groups are, like their ministers, inclined to find compromises on the proposals of the Commission and to bring home results. This result-oriented approach of civil servants does not seem to be a good mechanism to control the competences of the EU. To be fair, my experience with working groups taught me that the issue of subsidiarity was raised on occasion, but it was always raised by a representative that opposed a certain proposal because of policy reasons. Thus, it was always raised in an opportunistic way linked with a political view on the substance of the proposal.

Often, in the initial stage of legislation before the commission tables a proposal to the EP and to the Council, experts are invited by the Commission to make comments on draft proposals of the Commission. National experts, in many cases again civil servants, are so proud to be invited by the Commission that they dare not raise questions of subsidiarity or proportionality. So, these experts, at the initial stage, do not function at all as a check on the powers of the EU.

At last, the Court of Justice has a task in guarding the attribution of powers to the EU and the guarding of the principle of subsidiarity. However, roughly speaking, the Court always interpreted the attribution of powers very broadly.[4] Not surprisingly, the Court seemed to have its own agenda in favouring an expansion of powers conferred on the EU and on the integration of the EU.

---

3 See Advice Council of State of 15 September 2005 on improvement of the Dutch participation in EU decision-making, Kamerstukken II 2005/06, 29 993, no. 22 and no. 27.

4 Hancher & Van den Brink, p. 2808.

So far, we have found only forces inclined to expand the competences of the EU. Are national parliaments able to play a countervailing power in judging not only competences but also the use of those competences?

3 Yellow and Orange Cards

The contribution of national parliaments to the principle of subsidiarity is mentioned for the first time in the Treaty of Lisbon (Article 12 consolidated version of the Treaty on European Union). This contribution is spelled out in nine articles of Protocol No. 2, 'On the application of the principles of subsidiarity and proportionality.' Article 6 determines that any national parliament may, within eight weeks from the date of transmission of a draft legislative act, send to the Presidents of the European Parliament, the Council and the Commission a reasoned opinion stating why it considers that the draft in question does not comply with the principle of subsidiarity. It will be for each national parliament or each chamber of a national parliament to consult, where appropriate, regional parliaments with legislative powers.

Article 7, subsection 2 reads: *'Where reasoned opinions on a draft legislative acts' non-compliance with the principle of subsidiarity represent at least one third of all the votes allocated to the national Parliaments in accordance with the second subparagraph of paragraph 1, the draft must be reviewed. This threshold shall be a quarter in the case of a draft legislative act submitted [...] on the area of freedom, security and justice'.* After such review, the Commission has to reconsider the draft but may maintain, amend or withdraw the draft. Reasons must be given for this decision. This procedure is known as the yellow card procedure. This procedure was already part of the draft Constitutional Treaty.

The orange card procedure is a new procedure added to the yellow card procedure.

Article 7, subparagraph 3 reads: *'Furthermore, under the ordinary legislative procedure, where reasoned opinions on the non-compliance of a proposal for a legislative act with the principle of subsidiarity represent at least a simple majority of the votes allocated to national Parliament [...] the proposal must be reviewed.'*

Article 7, 3,(b) reads; *' if, by a majority of the members of the Council or a majority of the votes cast in the European parliament, the legislator is of the opinion that the proposal is not compatible with the principle of subsidiarity, the legislative proposal shall not be given further consideration.'*

Although the Netherlands government was in favour of having a red card procedure during the negotiations about the Lisbon Treaty, this proved to be a bridge too far.[5] Now the procedure of the orange card is considered by the Dutch government as a major breakthrough and as a real brake on the use of powers of

5 Prof. Dr. A.T.J.M. Jacobs, 'Het Verdrag van Lissabon en de Europese grondwet, Is er een 'overtuigend onderscheid'?', *NJB* 2008, p. 327.

the EU.[6] However, the question remains whether national parliaments can play such an important role.

4 The Constitutional Position of National Parliaments

In the Treaty of Lisbon, national parliaments are mentioned for the first time in the text of the treaty itself. In Article 12, national parliaments are given specified tasks: 'national Parliaments *shall* [in italics by author] contribute actively to the good functioning of the Union'. It is important to note that here the word '*shall*' is used and not the word '*may*'. So in fact, this task is formulated as a duty and not as a possibility. This main task is further specified in seven subtasks. National parliaments will be informed, seeing to things, taking part in evaluation mechanisms, will be notified; but they will have no teeth other than in facilitating the function of the Union. Some British members of the House of Commons have asked themselves the question whether, as national parliamentarians, they have the duty to serve the Union instead of serving the interests of their own state.[7] '*The legal judgment of our officials is that that will be used by the ECJ to say that the Commission, if it wishes to in future, can take infraction against any Parliament that refuses to participate in a part of the EU's institutions*'.[8]

Is it not strange that national parliaments get their tasks from the EU, instead of their national constitutions? Of course, there is the precedent that national courts are given tasks by treaties. However, it makes a difference in so far that national courts are assigned European tasks in the execution of European law while national parliaments are given European law-making duties.[9] They contribute to the lawmaking function in the EU. This top-down exercise is inconsistent with the way most national parliaments gained their powers, often conquered at the cost of other national organs like kings and governments. Mostly, those powers were earned through a struggle to establish a parliamentary system where ministers are accountable to their parliament.

The House of Commons European Scrutiny Committee commented that Article 12 of the Lisbon Treaty should not be formulated as an obligation, and it is wholly a matter for a national parliament to decide whether it wishes to use these opportunities. '*National parliaments, unlike the European Parliament, are not creations of the Treaties and their rights are not dependent on them. In our view,*

---

6 W.J.M. Voermans, 'Invloed van nationale parlementen op Europese wetgeving: hoe doen de buren dat?', *RegelMaat*, 2007/4, p. 155.

7 See for example: Ms Gisela Stuart, (Birmingham, Edgbaston) (Lab), House of Commons publications, Common Hansard, debate, 26 July 2007.

8 Michael Connarty (Chairman of the European Scrutiny Committee), House of Commons publications, Common Hansard debates 11 December 2007.

9 Kiiver, p. 186.

the imposition of such a legal duty on the Parliament of this country is objectionable as a matter of principle and must be resisted.'[10]

In any case, it is clear from the place and function attributed by the Treaty of Lisbon to national parliaments, that one can no longer speak of the EU and the Member States as two separate legal orders. The structure of the constitutional order of the EU is interwoven with the national constitutional order. Kiiver seems to regret that fact as he writes in his dissertation: 'The third flaw lies in the depiction of parliaments as unitary institutions [...].'[11] Besselink even concludes that there is only one legal order, consisting of the constitution of the EU and the constitutions of the Member States and that one cannot speak of a hierarchy between the constitutional legal order of the EU and those of the Member States.[12] Others like the Council of State of the Netherlands speak about the decision-making process in the EU as an interactive network organization.[13]

5 Do National Parliaments Exist?

National parliamentary control of EU decision-making is conceived as a counterbalance to the legislative competences that have been transferred to the EU level.[14]

One wonders if such a system, which attributes the role of primary watchdog of the principle of subsidiarity and proportionality to the national parliaments, is satisfactory. Parliaments consist of political parties. Some parties in principle support the government; they often form coalitions with other parties in supporting the government. Other parties oppose the government; they want to get rid of a certain government or cabinet. Can these political parties detach themselves from the content of the legislative proposal and only judge the proposal from the perspective of subsidiarity and vice versa? Can they distance themselves from political opportunism and is it fair to expect them to do so?

Parliaments are filled with politicians. These, logically, will look at their voters in answering questions of subsidiarity. Can they explain to their voters that they are very much against the content of the proposal in question but that they have no objections from the perspective of the principle of subsidiarity? Are we not expecting too much from the national politicians? Besides, in parliaments where coalition-parties have to find compromises in order to find a majority in parliament, the question of subsidiarity will be dealt with along the lines of party politics. A compromise on the issue of a principle has to be

---

10 Report of the European Scrutiny Report, p. 24.

11 Kiiver, 2006, p. 187.

12 L.F.M. Besselink, *A Composite European Constitution, Inaugurural lecture*, Europa Law Publishing, Groningen 2007.

13 Advice Council of State of 15 September 2005 Kamerstukken II 2005/06, 29 993, no. 22 and no. 27.

14 Olaf Tans, in *National Parliaments and European Democracy*, edited by Olaf Tans, Carla Zoethout and Jit Peters, Europa Law Publishing 2007, p. 235.

found within eight weeks. That seems to be a too short period to understand the merits of the proposal and to discuss it and to consult regional parliaments if they feel the need. These regional parliaments also need time to study, discuss and compromise.

Tans argues convincingly that relations between political parties in parliament and the government are governed by the constitutional principle of ministerial responsibility.[15] Ministers can be called to account and be held responsible for their conduct and their subordinates and must resign when a vote of non-confidence is passed in parliament. One can say that national parliamentary control of EU decision-making is also based on the idea of ministerial responsibility. Ministers have to justify and explain their actions in the Council to national parliaments. So far, I am unfamiliar with votes of no confidence in relation to actions or votes of ministers in the Council.

However, the resignation of ministers forms only part of the principle of ministerial responsibility. Parliaments tend to accept that ministers have limited control and can only be held accountable as far as they had a fair chance to exert influence. Ministers are, by lack of transparency of the decision-making process in the Council, able to blame others for the compromises that are eventually reached and the defeats they have been suffering. So, in national parliaments, ministerial responsibility dominates the relations between political parties and government and dominates often the debate in parliament. This raises the question if ministerial responsibility is a satisfactory normative cornerstone to influence questions about subsidiarity and EU policy in general by national parliaments.[16]

6 Subsidiarity as Political Principle

The principle of subsidiarity is not new; it was introduced by the Treaty of Maastricht in 1992. However, until now it has only served as a symbolic principle. The decision makers in Brussels paid it lip service, but it did not play an essential role a brake on legislative actions. The courts only reviewed the procedure and the reasoning for policy measures in a very marginal way.[17]

Could the Court have done more? Probably not. There is a general feeling amongst legal scholars that we are dealing here with a 'political' principle, i.e. a principle of which the enforcement essentially must be in the hands of political institutions. The role of the courts in enforcing it can only be a limited one.[18]

---

15 Tans, p. 228-231.

16 Tans, 2007, p. 240.

17 Court of Justice, 12-11-1996, C-491/01; Court of Justice, 13-05-1997, C-233/94; Court of Justice, 10-12-2002, C-491/01.

18 L.A. Geelhoed, 'Een Europawijde Europese Unie: een grondwet zonder staat?', *SEW* 9 (2003), p. 196; R. Barents, 'Naar een Europese Constitutie? (VI)', *NTER* 2003, p. 221-222; T. Koopmans, 'De Europese Conventie-een tussenstand', *SEW* 6, (2003), p. 196. It is interesting to compare the role of the European

Subsidiarity is a concept that cannot easily be isolated from substantive criteria. It is far more of a political than a legal nature.[19] Although the Protocol on the application of the principles of subsidiarity and proportionality ultimately still leaves room for judicial interference (Article 8), it clearly recognises the political character of the principle of subsidiarity by attributing a primary supervising role to national parliaments.

On the other hand, the Treaty and the Protocol seem to deal with the principle of subsidiarity as if it is a neutral and objective principle. The Protocol for example does require from national parliaments a reasoned opinion stating why it considers that the draft in question does not comply with the principle of subsidiarity.[20] Generally speaking, courts are used to giving reasoned opinions, parliaments are not. Every party in parliament has its own political reasons.

The *ex ante* review of proposals from the Commission is a cumbersome task for parliamentarians. Previous experience shows that those *ex ante* screening mechanisms are employed selectively.[21] It otherwise leads to an overload of work, due to the sheer volume of European documents to be processed – under pressure of time – by national parliaments.[22] Parliaments are not at their best in exercising routine mechanisms of a technical nature. They are not suited to play this kind of inspectorial role. Members of parliament would rather spend their time in involvement in short-term national issues that attract the attention of the voters. Those parliamentarians who are interested in re-election should not become too involved in subsidiarity questions.

7 Other Countervailing Powers?

However, so far, I do not see other political institutions that might play an essential role as countervailing power to the expansion of the EU. As things are now, we must hope that national parliaments will take their role as the watchdog of subsidiarity seriously and that the Commission, the European Parliament and the Council will take their objections seriously. Then the principle of subsidiarity, as elaborated in the Protocol, might gain some teeth in which case the Treaty of Lisbon will, in this respect, not be considered as an opportunity wasted. That might help to enhance the democratic legitimacy of the European Union.

courts in upholding the principle of subsidiarity with the role of the Supreme Court in the United States in protecting the Interstate Commerce Clause at the time of the New Deal under President Franklin Roosevelt, which almost led to a constitutional crisis.

19 Kiiver, 2006, p. 188.

20 See for example Article 6 and Article 7, 2 of the Protocol.

21 See Evaluatie Tijdelijke Commissie Subsidiariteitstoets, Staten-Generaal, 2006-2007, 30 953, C and nr. 3, p. 5.

22 Tans, p. 240.

When the majority of national parliaments opposes certain proposals from the perspective of subsidiarity, it is difficult to imagine that such a proposal will nevertheless become law.[23] However, national parliaments will then have the burdensome task of organizing themselves and forming a majority, all within a period of eight weeks. This is only thinkable in cases of political incidents that attract great public attention, like the Directive on Services.

One might expect that national parliaments would be interested in guarding their own competences, especially in the field of legislation. Where their role as guardians of subsidiarity will be combined with their role as controller of national executive power, there might be an opportunity for national parliaments to play a relevant role in this respect. This guardianship must also be interwoven with a role in leading a debate that is relevant on the national political stage.[24] In other words: The role of national parliaments in guarding the principle of subsidiarity must on the European stage be linked with the 'regular' parliamentarian role on the national stage of controlling ministers and holding ministers accountable; the so called ex post parliamentary procedure.

But that is not enough. Many parliaments go beyond this by trying to influence the decision-making on the EU level, through procedures like the 'scrutiny reserve' and 'mandating' procedures that are in place in many Member States of the EU.[25] Under '*scrutiny reserve*', it is understood that ministers should not agree to EU proposals in the Council until parliamentary scrutiny has been completed. Under '*mandating procedure*', it is understood that ministers are only to act and adopt negotiating positions under the binding instructions of parliament. I think that the principle of subsidiarity might be given real meaning if it would be coupled with a procedure similar to a '*scrutiny reserve*' or a '*mandating procedure*'. One should not have the illusion that the principle of subsidiarity can be separated from the substance of proposals.

8 Parliamentary Procedure on Subsidiarity in The Netherlands

Since 2006, the parliament in The Netherlands has set up a Temporary Committee on Review of Subsidiarity. The Committee is a so-called joint committee consisting of members from the Second Chamber (the lower house) and members of the First Chamber (the senate).

Joint committee's are exceptional in The Netherlands. Recently the functioning of this committee was evaluated by the parliament itself.[26] Two interesting facts from that report are worth mentioning here. First of all, only twelve proposals were reviewed out of a number of more than two hundred propos-

[23] 20 Jacobs, p. 328.

[24] Dr. O. Tans, 'De oranje kaart: een nieuwe rol voor nationale parlementen?', *SEW* 2007, p. 445 and 446.

[25] Voermans, p. 157-160.

[26] Evaluatie Tijdelijke Commissie Subsidiariteitstoets, Staten-Generaal 2006-2007, 30 953, C and nr. 3.

als.[27] The Committee was not able to cope with more proposals due to the lack of staff aiding the Committee with its task. To cope with more proposals, the Committee recommended additional funds to attract more staff. The Committee complained that the active participation of members of the Second Chamber was not optimal and needed improvement.[28]

Four of the twelve proposals reviewed were objected to. An interesting debate on the merits of the objections as to competences took place with the European Commission. However, the Commission persisted and was eventually successful.

The Committee complained that it was hard within the framework of the COSAC to decide on experimenting on subsidiarity review of more than two proposals only.[29] It seemed also difficult to interest other national parliaments in the objections of The Netherlands as to the four proposals. The Committee recommended closer cooperation between national parliaments.

Secondly, Van Dijk, the chairman of the Committee, showed in an article describing the functioning of the Committee that the judgment on subsidiarity was highly coloured by political reasons. A good example forms the judgment on a proposal of a directive on soil-protection. The Committee did not see any problem with the subsidiarity issue of this proposal. It asked also the opinion of the standing Committee on Environment (VROM commissie). This last committee showed great objections as to the proposal. But all these objections were politically motivated.[30] Even Dutch lobbying employers' organizations objected for political reasons to the proposal on soil protection, but environmental non-governmental organizations welcomed the proposal. At last, for tactical reasons, it decided not to send the subsidiarity objections to the EU institutions but only to the own government. Van Dijk even named this procedure on only informing the own government about the subsidiarity objections, a new instrument.[31] The government sent through a so-called 'fiche procedure' comments on new proposals of the EU to parliament. It made also known to parliament its judgment as to subsidiarity. The government so far had almost no objections to mention as to subsidiarity.[32]

The largest party in the Second Chamber, the CDA, took it upon itself to formulate future criteria in selecting proposals for review on the principle of subsidiarity. Three of the five criteria they formulated (namely the scope of the proposal; the consequences of the proposal for The Netherlands; the political sensitivity of the proposal) are clearly political criteria, which have nothing to do with the principle of subsidiarity or proportionality.[33]

---

27 Evaluation Report, p. 5 and Van Dijk, 'Hoe verging het de Tijdelijke Commissie Subsidiariteitstoets (TCS)?', p. 146.

28 Evaluation Report, p. 7.

29 Van Dijk, p. 142.

30 Van Dijk, p. 143.

31 Van Dijk, p. 144.

32 Hancher & Van den Brink, p. 2809.

33 Van Dijk, p. 148.

9 Strengthening National Parliaments

As to competences under the so-called third pillar of the EU, the Dutch parliament, the Second Chamber as well as the First Chamber, had reserved for themselves under the approval legislation of the Maastricht Treaty a kind of *'scrutiny reserve'* procedure. The reason for this *'approval procedure'* is the limited role the European Parliament is playing in these matters. So, the intention was to fill in a democratic gap. Parliament reserved for itself a *'right of approval'*.

Firstly, draft proposals had to be made public. Secondly, these proposals were to be put before parliament. Thirdly, the approval of parliament had to be required before ministers could bind The Netherlands in the decision-making process.[34]

During the approval procedure of the Lisbon Treaty, which is now under way, the government has taken the view that the *'approval procedure'* under the existent third pillar does not serve any interest in matters where the European Parliament will be given the right of co-decision and the Council can decide with qualified majority. The 'Standing committee of experts on international immigration, refugee and criminal law', an advisory committee to the government, strongly disagrees with the government. It recommends maintaining the procedure of 'approval' even for matters under co-decision or qualified majority. Parliamentary input is useful during the stage of negotiations in the Council and national parliaments are in a better position to influence their own ministers.[35] As Erik Jurgens, former member of the Second and First Chamber reasoned, the European Parliament lacks the power to hold members of the Council accountable for their actions in the Council.[36]

An active input of the national parliament is at stake here. National parliaments are not in competition with the EP but are an addendum to the EU decision-making process. They are better to fulfil their obligations under the Lisbon Treaty with a more active input than only a judgment on subsidiarity.

A good example is the letter written of the 'Standing committee on the Justice Council of the First Chamber' of the Dutch Parliament to the State Secretary of Justice.[37] Because the proposed *'Directive of the European Parliament and of the Council on common standards and procedures in Member States for returning illegally staying third-country nationals'* does not fall under the *'approval procedure'*, parliamentarians complain that they do not get any information about the ongoing negotiations from the government. That would be altogether different if the proposed directive would fall under the *'approval procedure'*.

---

34 See for this procedure: Standing committee of experts on international immigration, refugee and criminal law, Advice, January 3 2008, CM08001-1.

35 See above, p. 3 and 4.

36 E.C.M. Jurgens, *Een onparlementair stelsel*, Inaugural Lecture Maastricht, 1993, p. 15-19.

37 Letter March 4-2008, 140890.u/PB/KvD.

10 Conclusions

Are there enough checks on the ever-growing expansion of powers of the EU? The EC, EP and the Council all have a tendency to expand the competences of the EU. The role of national parliaments, using yellow cards and orange cards as to the question of subsidiarity and proportionality, does not carry enough weight to counterbalance all these powers.

The attribution of the competence of guarding the principle of subsidiarity to national parliaments neglects the fact that national parliaments consist of political parties supporting the government or opposing the government. Their views will always be coloured by political reasons. The principle of subsidiarity is therefore not a technical, neutral principle, but in essence a political principle. It is rather artificial to separate the principle of subsidiarity and proportionality from the substance of the related proposals.

On the other hand, we might expect national parliaments to care about their own legislative competences. When the guarding of the principle of subsidiarity is linked with the political role of national parliaments as controllers of government and national legislators, national parliaments may play a more important role as a check on the EU. This function might be enhanced when national parliaments review subsidiarity by means of procedures such as *'scrutiny reserve'* and *'mandating procedures'*, with which many national parliaments are already familiar. The principle of subsidiarity and proportionality are not static but dynamic concepts, in the sense that during negotiations in the Council, proposals might be amended in a way that cannot been foreseen within eight weeks of the tabling of a new proposal. Therefore, in fact, subsidiarity and proportionality should constantly be reviewed during the negotiations.

National parliaments should not be seen as competition to the European Parliament but as a fellow player with a different role. National parliaments should also not be activated in an unnatural role as a kind of inspectorate. They should be activated in a way that suits them, and that allows them to be at their best. That means that their function as EU players should be linked to their national traditions and not the other way around.

National parliaments are strongest when they judge proposals on their political merits on an incidental basis. In that sense, they may also attract political attention from the media and the citizens. It is easier, in a national debate, to communicate a political problem than a technical one like subsidiarity. When we fully recognize this fact, and do not overestimate the role of national parliaments in EU matters, they may fulfil more important functions. These functions do not ask for a continuous influx of parliamentary viewpoints in the decision-making process of the EU. 'Rather they ask for the creation of incidents; specific moments on which specific issues are politicized or legally disputed'.[38]

Sometimes national parliaments should be able to give red cards to a proposal of the EU. If national parliaments may only give orange and yellow

[38] Tans, *National Parliaments and European Democracy*, p. 245.

cards, but not red cards, the citizens would lose their respect for national parliaments, and that is already not too high.

Strengthening the position of national parliaments may not only function as a countervailing power in a system of checks and balances; it might also have the side effect of enhancing the legitimization of the decision-making of the EU. However, relatively active and strong parliaments in EU policymaking are no means of bridging the gap between citizens and the EU as the examples of Great Britain and Denmark show. However, that is an altogether different issue.

CHAPTER 4

Accountability to National Parliaments in the European Union

Philipp Kiiver

It is my pleasure to respond to the very clear and thoughtful speech by Jit Peters. It gives me an opportunity to comment not only on Prof. Peters' contribution itself, but also, more generally, on the excellent edited volume, which he recently published together with Olaf Tans and Carla Zoethout.[1]

My response comprises two elements. The first deals with the *democratic dimension* of accountability to national parliaments in the context of the European Union. I applaud Prof. Peters for drawing a clear distinction on this point, and for approaching the subject from a *checks and balances* perspective rather than from a democratic legitimacy perspective. My second point concerns the divide between legal and inter-disciplinary methodology, which I will discuss further below.

1 Democracy versus Checks and Balances

All too often, the democracy aspect of accountability to parliaments is taken to be the first and foremost purpose of such accountability relationships in the context of the European Union. The natural – but misleading – implication is then that, by virtue of being democratically elected, members of parliament increase the democratic content of whatever activity they engage in. Thus, the greater the extent to which national parliamentarians are involved in European decision-making processes, the more democratic the processes themselves would automatically become. This logic is nowhere spelt out in quite the same crassness, but it does underlie many an argument in political discourse and in the literature where national parliaments are introduced to provide a remedy to the European Union's 'democratic deficit'.

Democracy is not the only dimension of accountability, however. In the typology developed by Mark Bovens, the democratic rationale of accountability regimes is indeed one of the notion's aspects, but it is not the only one.[2] For example, accountability to a forum may be desirable from a learning perspective, improving the quality of decision-making by making it subject to external assessment. Yet such process would not need to be democratic in nature.

The focus on checks and balances as the defining dimension in Prof. Peters' line of research is, again, to be hailed as a positive choice. For in the context of the European Union, the very existence of oversight by institutions that are not identical to the governments – namely national parliaments – is already a precious asset. The fact that within their Member States, parliaments represent the core of the democratic character of their constitution may be seen as an added value but not as the decisive value. To illustrate this point: it would be inconsistent to define national parliamentary activity in terms of their demo-

1 O. Tans, C. Zoethout and J. Peters, eds, *National Parliaments and European Democracy; A Bottom-up Approach to European Constitutionalism* (Groningen: Europa Law Publishing, 2007).

2 See M. Bovens, 'Analysing and Assessing Public Accountability: A Conceptual Framework', 2006 *European Governance Papers*, no. C-06-01.

cratic properties while at the same time applauding scrutiny of EU policy by the unelected House of Lords. Also, the Dutch upper house has a fine record of EU-related monitoring activity, but it remains a chamber that is but indirectly elected.

What is of at least equal importance here – compared to the fact that (lower chambers of) parliaments are directly elected – is the extent to which such parliaments may foster politicization of EU issues. On this count, upper chambers again have an important contribution to make. Whether they are directly elected, indirectly elected, or not elected at all, chambers of national parliaments usually have the capacity to capture public attention and to galvanize public debate.

Deliberative capacity is therefore another important asset that parliaments hold, next to their already mentioned capacity to exercise checks and balances vis-à-vis the executive. None of this is necessarily equal to democratic legitimacy.

2 An Inter-Disciplinary Research Agenda

The second point I should like to raise concerns the focus Prof. Peters is putting, in his contribution and in his edited volume, on the formal prerogatives of parliaments, in the sense of a disposition of power as a matter of positive law.

Of course, as legal scholars, we are well-advised to devote attention to the legal aspect of political relations in a constitutional set-up. This is where we are able to produce solid and enlightening findings, as Prof. Peters and his colleagues have done in their edited volume. The inherently stricter attention of legal scholars to the scope and formulation of written and unwritten rules is also where they have a comparative advantage over other disciplines.

Nevertheless, in a field such as this one, I suggest to complement this strictly legal perspective with a more inter-disciplinary view. Apart from providing an inventory and a critical analysis of what powers national parliaments hold in the context of EU decision-making, it would also be of utmost relevance to see how reforms to national parliamentary involvement in the EU can stimulate the use of powers that they already have. In other words, it would not only be important to see what new powers would be given to national parliaments by, for example, the Treaty of Lisbon – that list would be mostly disappointing.[3] It is also important to see how the political momentum of having these new procedures in the first place, such as a notionally reinforced Early Warning System for the principle of subsidiarity, can translate into increased 'European awareness' among parliamentarians. For this purpose, I draw an analytical distinction between the *constitutive* value and the *catalytic* value of parliament-friendly EU treaty provi-

[3] Ph. Kiiver, 'The Treaty of Lisbon, the National Parliaments and the Principle of Subsidiarity', 15 *Maastricht Journal of European and Comparative Law* (2008) pp. 77-83.

sions.[4] The former is clearly a matter for legal research (what are the powers given to parliaments), while the latter would also take into account how public debate can make EU policy more salient, and thereby press politicians into becoming more pro-active in that field.

I completely agree with Prof. Paul Craig who, in his oral intervention, pointed out that an institution's effective use of power cannot be separated from the amount of power that is actually available. It is therefore exactly my ambition to show that national parliamentarians already have the necessary tools at their disposal, most of them as a matter of domestic constitutional law: ministerial accountability, the right to access to information, the possibility to engage in dialogues with EU institutions and with other national parliaments. What future research might now actually attempt to show is to what extent developments such as EU treaty reform prompt parliamentarians to make more and better use of the powers they already have.

4 Ibid.

CHAPTER 5

Political Accountability: A Useful Concept in EU Inter-Institutional Relations?

Luc Verhey

1 Introduction

We go back to the fall of 2004, more than four years ago, when, For the first time in history, the European Parliament came close to refusing the Commission as proposed by its president Barroso. The *de facto* rejection of the Commission by the Parliament can be seen as a new step forward towards new constitutional relationships in the European Union. The claim expressed in 2004 and confirmed by the Reform Treaty that the President, and the composition of the entire Commission, should reflect the composition of Parliament,[1] may not only mark the development of a new constitutional practice in the formation of a Commission, but more general the introduction at the European level of a regime which comes again a bit closer to a parliamentary regime.

The events in 2004 remind us also of the fall of the Santer Commission in 1999.[2] As is well-known, the first report of the Committee of Independent Experts at the time led to the collective resignation of the Santer Commission, before the Parliament could come to a vote. However, from a constitutional perspective, the second report of the Committee was even more important.[3] It concluded that the concept of political accountability at the European level remained unclear and that mechanisms for its practical application remained inadequate.

It is interesting to see that the Committee explicitly linked its observations to developments at the national level. It recognised that there are important differences in the constitutional systems of the EU Member States as to the precise form of ministerial accountability and that the position of the European Parliament could not be assimilated entirely with that of a national parliament. Yet, this did not prevent:

'national parliaments from serving as a model, insofar as they reveal constitutional characteristics which may increasingly also shape the role of the European Parliament'.[4]

This point was further developed by Walter van Gerven, member of the Committee of Independent Experts, in a guest editorial in the *Common Market Law Review*, when he wrote (I quote):

'It will be obvious that many of the issues touched upon in the first and the second report (..) raise constitutional questions which the legal orders of the Member States have in common. This is therefore an area where comparative research would be particularly helpful in uncovering common principles, which would in turn help in

1 Article 17 (7) TEU, as supposed to be amended by the Reform Treaty.

2 See for more details A. Tomkins, 'Responsibility and resignation in the European Commission', *MLR* 1999, p. 744 ff.

3 Committee of Independent Experts, Second report on the Reform of the Commission, Analysis of current practice and proposals for tackling mismanagement, irregularities and fraud, Brussels 1999

4 Committee of Independent Experts, Second report, op. cit., p. 129, nr. 7.14.2.

designing constitutional rules for the European Union – with account being taken, of course, of the peculiarities of the Union's legal order.'[5]

This search for common principles is not a goal in itself; it could contribute to winning the support of the people for the European Union. The parliamentary systems, as they operate at the national level, create the expectation in the minds of many that when at the European level real decisions are taken that influence their lives directly; this can only be done by accountable government, by institutions which must give account of their actions to the people's representatives in parliament, and which may ultimately have to step down when mistakes have been made.

This is in a nutshell why it is useful to have a closer look to national experiences with regard to the issue of political accountability. This way of looking at institutional relationships in the EU is new; it is a type of research that has never really been conducted in a comprehensive manner.[6] Arguments have often been used on whether national experiences are useful or not.[7] However, they are based on assumptions: they have never really and systematically been checked. Therefore it is important to focus in a more systematic way on national experiences on political accountability. Could these experiences lead to the further development of a European concept of accountability?

---

5 W. van Gerven, Guest Editorial, 'Ethical and political responsibility of EU Commissioners', *CMLRev.* 2000, p. 6. More elaborate W. van Gerven, op. cit., p. 81 ff and 309 ff.

6 See P. Craig and A. Tomkins (eds.), *The Executive and Public Law. Power and Accountability in Comparative Perspective*, Oxford University Press 2006, 355 ff. We can agree with their statement that 'public law research into the nature of executive power is only just beginning' (p. 15).

7 In discussing solutions of the EU's 'democratic deficit' authors, while recognizing that the EU is not a traditional state, often explicitly or implicitly seem to fall back on or let themselves be inspired by national models of representative democracy. Perhaps the clearest example is W. van Gerven, *The European Union. A Polity of States and Peoples*, Hart Publishing Oxford 2005, 397 ff. See further P. Dann, 'European Parliament and Executive Federalism: Approaching a Parliament in a Semi-Parliamentary Democracy', *ELJ* 2003, 549 ff, B. Crum, 'Tailoring Representative Democracy to the European Union: Does the European Constitution Reduce the Democratic Deficit?', *ELJ* 2005, 452 ff and A. Follesdal and S. Hix, 'Why There is a Democratic Deficit in the EU: A Response to Majone and Moravcsik', *European Governance Papers (EUROGOV)* 2005. No. C-05-02, http:/www.connex-network.org/eurogov/pdf/egp-connex-C-05-02.pdf. Other authors however criticize traditional nation-state oriented ways of constitutional thinking and argue for new forms of constitutionalism. See for instance M.P. Maduro, Europe and the constitution: what if this is as good as it gets, in J.H.H. Weiler and M. Wind (eds), *European Constitutionalism Beyond the State*, Cambridge University Press (2003), 73 ff. and other contributions in the same volume.

2 Political Accountability: Two Basic Models

Summarizing the general picture we can say that the concept of political accountability has a longstanding tradition, at least in the Member States of EU-15. Its origins are closely tied to the rise of the parliamentary system in the nineteenth century or even further back. In the new Member States, the transformation into a parliamentary system has taken place after the fall of communism. In most cases, they copied more or less one of the existing models in Western Europe. Given this fact, one can safely conclude that all the Member States have a parliamentary system[8] in which the executive is usually held accountable through the concept of ministerial accountability. This concept is nowadays still seen as an essential element of democratic government in all the Member States.

Accordingly, at this abstract level there seems to be some sort of 'ius commune' in Europe. However, taking a closer look, it is much more difficult to identify precisely confined principles and practices common in all the systems involved. The rules and principles based on constitutional theory vary widely in the Member States. Evidently, this variety is closely connected with the historical, political and constitutional nature of each and every national system.

Roughly speaking, one can say that there are two basic models of political accountability in the Member States: the 'parliament-oriented' and the 'government-oriented' model. Both models focus on the relationship between the government and the parliament, which is crucial in every parliamentary system. However, the perspective of both models is different.[9]

3 The 'Parliament-Oriented' Model

In the so-called 'parliament-oriented' model, which is in place in the majority of the Member States, political accountability is essentially about the confidence the parliamentary majority must have in the government. If at a certain moment this confidence appears to be no longer there, political accountability means primarily the acceptance of political consequences: the government (or an individual minister) must step down. In some parliamentary systems, like

8 See for France Jacques Ziller, 'Political Accountability in France', in: Luc Verhey, Hansko Broeksteeg and Ilse Van den Driessche (eds.), *Political Accountability in Europe: Which Way Forward. A Traditional Concept of Parliamentary Democracy in an EU Context*, Europa Law Publishing, Groningen 2008, p. 81 ff.

9 See more elaborate Hansko Broeksteeg, Ilse van den Driessche and Luc Verhey, 'Political accountability in the EU Member States: Different Concepts and Practical Implications', in: Luc Verhey, Hansko Broeksteeg and Ilse Van den Driessche (eds.), op. cit., p. 271 ff.

in Italy[10] and Spain,[11] this 'parliament-oriented' concept of political accountability directly relates to the constitutional theory of popular sovereignty. As being regarded as the voice of the people, the parliament must be dominant over the government in order to guarantee the latter's democratic legitimacy. So at the end of the day, the parliament must have the tools to let the government do what the people want it to do and if not, to force the government to resign.

If we try to transform this model towards the European Union, we run up against major obstacles. In the system of the European Union, democratic legitimacy is based on more than one source: next to the European Parliament there is the Council of Ministers as well as the European Council which are considered to be representing the Member States and, at least indirectly, the people from the Member States. As a result, the European Parliament cannot be regarded as the one and only 'bearer' of democratic legitimacy, at least not in the way as it is deemed to be the case in national parliamentary systems.[12] The dual source of democratic legitimacy within the European Union finds expression for example in the way the Commission has been appointed. Different from national governments the composition of the Commission is not the direct and immediate result of the elections for the European Parliament. It is the outcome of a complicated procedure in which the European Parliament has influence but the Member States at the end of the day still seem to have the final say.

The absence of a singular source of democratic legitimacy within the European Union has consequences in terms of political accountability. Applying the 'parliament-oriented' concept of political accountability, as described earlier, is in the European context not obvious. From a democratic perspective, the European Parliament seems to be less legitimized to dismiss one or more members of the executive than for example the British, the Polish or the Italian Parliament. This is not to say that the European Parliament should not have the power to send away the Commission as established in article 201 EC-Treaty. This power is a necessary tool in order to realize effective institutional checks and balances at the European level. But, whether it is necessary from a democratic perspective is another matter,[13] In the present European Union, the European Parliament, although being elected, cannot claim the final say.

---

10 Lorenza Violini, Stefania Ninatti and Giulia Tiberi, 'Political Accountability in Italy', in Luc Verhey, Hansko Broeksteeg and Ilse Van den Driessche (eds.), op. cit., p. 121 ff.

11 Enoch Alberti, 'Political Accountability in Spain', in Luc Verhey, Hansko Broeksteeg and Ilse Van den Driessche (eds.), op. cit., p. 211ff.

12 We leave aside here whether or not Europe lacks the *demos* which according to some authors is indispensable for the functioning of the democratic system. In this sense D. Grimm, 'Does Europe need a Constitution', *ELJ* 1995, p. 282. See also W. van Gerven, *The European Union. A Polity of States and Peoples*, Hart Publishing Oxford 2005, 41 ff.

13 See for an uncoupling of accountability and democracy also D. Chalmers, C. Hadjiemmanuil, G. Monti, A. Tomkins, *EU Law. Text and Materials*, Cambridge University Press 2006, p. 313.

4 The 'Government-Oriented' Model of Political Accountability

At first sight, the second model of political accountability seems to fit better into the European picture. In this, what we have called the 'government-oriented' model, political accountability is not or not primarily about the consequences the government should take from a vote of censure by a parliamentary majority, but far more about what happens in the preceding phases. The basic questions are more governmental in nature such as for which public services the government is exactly accountable for, which powers the government actually has to give effect to its political accountability and how exactly the government has to give an account to parliament. The crucial issue here is the scope of the government's accountability and the quality of the mechanisms by which the government give an account.

Transforming this 'government-oriented' model towards the European Union seems possible. If we look at the Commission as the institution, which is politically accountable, similar issues seem to rise as in national systems. We could draw various parallels between the Commission and national governments; we could look at legal powers or other instruments to make their accountability effective; we could compare the relationship between the government or the Commission and executive and regulatory agencies; we could also focus on processes or mechanisms by which national governments give an account and look whether such processes or mechanisms could be applied in and around the Commission. At first sight, such an approach seems to be thinkable if not promising.

However, there is at least one preliminary question which has to be dealt with first and which seems to confront us with an insurmountable problem: can the Commission reasonably be regarded as a 'government'? At the European level there are effectively more institutions performing tasks of an executive nature. The European Union has what is called a 'dual executive' where on the one hand the Council of Ministers and/or the European Council and on the other hand, the Commission share executive responsibilities[14]. In this context, it is essential that the Council is not only an institution of the European Union, but also, or perhaps even primarily, consists of representatives of the Member States who are accountable on the national level in the first place.

Thus, we cannot separate the relationship between the Parliament and the Commission from the context of the EU institutional framework as a whole. Authors like Magnette have shown convincingly that interinstitutional tensions are much more governed by national divisions and technical reasoning than by classical majoritarian attitudes.[15] As a result the relationship between the

[14] D. Curtin, *Mind the Gap: the Evolving EU Executive and the Constitution*, Europa Law Publishing, Groningen 2004.

[15] P. Magnette, 'Appointing and Censuring the European Commission: The Adaptation of Parliamentary Institutions to the Community Context', *European Law Journal* 2001, p. 292 ff.

Commission and the European Parliament is substantially different from that between a government and a parliament, as we know it in the Member States. Because they are both supranational institutions and share common interests, they are more often allies against the Council than enemies.

The conclusion from all this seems straightforward. Because the constitutional position of the Commission and the Council *vis-à-vis* the European Parliament is fundamentally different and the relationship between the Commission and the Parliament cannot be separated from the context of the EU institutional framework as a whole, the parallel with a full-fledged parliamentary system is only limited. The Commission cannot be identified as 'the' EU government. As a result, the possibility of transplanting the 'government-oriented' model of political accountability to the European Union seems to be limited as well.

5 General Principles of Accountability[16]

5.1 Why Could General Principles be Useful?

From the foregoing one could conclude that research into national concepts of political accountability has been rather useless. Some will probably say: very fine that you have more thoroughly checked that the concept of ministerial accountability cannot be transplanted towards the European level, but we could have told you that beforehand. So tell us: what's new?

A conclusion along these lines and just leaving it with that would be too simple. Here one has to distinguish between theory and practice. The fact that the European Union is not a parliamentary system and will not be in the foreseeable future does not mean that national rules and practices are meaningless. One could also look at accountability issues from a more practice-based perspective and see if and to what extent national rules or its underlying principles can have practical effect in the constitutional system of the European Union. Perhaps this could help improving present accountability mechanisms in daily practice and by this strengthening the checks and balances within the political system of the European Union.

So from this perspective the question would be: are their any basic rules or practices of accountability, which apply or could apply both on the national and on the European level? Taking into account the experiences and the debates about how political accountability in the Member States works in theory and in practice, at least six general guidelines can be identified. In a somewhat simplified way these can be formulated as follows:

- Be clear about what 'political accountability' exactly means (par. 5.2);
- Do not accept definitions aimed at evading accountability (par. 5.3);

[16] See more elaborate Luc Verhey, Monica Claes and Hansko Broeksteeg, 'Political Accountability in the European Union: Conceptual Analysis and Future Prospects', in: Luc Verhey, Hansko Broeksteeg and Ilse Van den Driessche (eds.), op. cit., p. 326 ff.

- Distinguish between collective and individual accountability (par. 5.4);
- Establish a clear chain of command (par. 5.5);
- Reduce fragmentation of the executive (par. 5.6);
- Do not focus on resignation, but on the quality of the account (par. 5.7).

Hereafter, I will very briefly explain why these guidelines could be important and what they could actual mean in the EU context.

5.2 A Clear Definition of Political Accountability

The first guideline is perhaps the most obvious one: be clear about what 'political accountability' exactly means. As we explained before, it is difficult to find a 'ius commune' in Europe, because the Member States use theoretically different models of political accountability. However, looking at daily practice, the picture seems to be easier to grip. If one tries to come to a synthesis, common features can be distinguished, which are explicitly or implicitly present in the practice of almost every parliamentary system. Summarized political accountability contains three basic elements:

- *being accountable:* the guarantee of the government being accountable to the parliament for the use of its executive powers;
- *calling into account*: the right of the parliament to call the government into account which results in the obligation of the government to inform the parliament and to explain and justify its conduct;
- *holding to account*: the right of the parliament to make a judgment on the conduct of the government which results in the obligation of the government to accept the consequences; this could ultimately mean resignation.

These elements are not new; they largely fit in with general accountability concepts as defined by others.[17] However, it can still help clarify the debate on political accountability in the European Union. This debate is often unclear or sometimes even evasive. If we look for example to the European Commission's White Paper on European Governance, 'accountability' is defined in a way that makes the concept almost meaningless. According to the Commission it means that:

'each of the EU Institutions must explain and take responsibility for what it does in Europe'.[18]

[17] See R. Mulgan, 'Accountability: An ever expanding concept?', *Public Administration* 2000, p. 555 ff, C. Harlow, *Accountability in the European Union*, Oxford: Oxford University Press 2002, p. 6 ff, D. Oliver, *Constitutional Reform in the UK*, Oxford: Oxford University Press 2003, p. 48, M. Bovens, 'Analysing and Assessing Public Accountability: A Conceptual Framework', *European Governance Papers* (EUROGOV), no. C-06-01, 2006, www.connex-network.org/eurogov. , p. 9. See further Luc Verhey and Monica Claes, 'Introduction: Political Accountability in an European Perspective', in: Luc Verhey, Hansko Broeksteeg and Ilse Van den Driessche (eds.), op. cit., p. 10 ff.

[18] European Commission, European Governance. A White Paper, COM (2001) 428 final, p. 10.

This definition raises questions. Who is exactly responsible for what? To whom and how are they are made responsible? What are the possible consequences of being responsible? The White Paper on European Governance did not give even the beginning of an answer on these questions. But where the Commission was totally silent about it in the first place was the political accountability of the Commission itself.

5.3 Evading Accountability

What regularly happens on both the national and the European level is that by choosing a limited definition, one tries to avoid accountability if something goes wrong. A well-known example is the distinction which was made by some British politicians between *accountability* and *responsibility*: ministers would be *accountable* in the way that they could be challenged about any action of the civil service, but they would only be *responsible* if they are directly and personally involved. Another example also from Britain is the refusal of ministers to take responsibility for management failures in executive agencies. In this view a minister would only be responsible for policy matters, not for operational concerns.[19] Britain is in this respect far from unique. Comparable arguments have occurred in for example the Netherlands[20] and Denmark.[21]

The same evasive conduct occurred in the run-up to the political crisis in the European Union in 1999. The Santer Commission stated that Commissioners were responsible only for matters of policy, and not for questions of implementation. The Committee of Independent Experts rightly argued that 'this distinction, if strictly interpreted, is tenable neither in law nor in fact'.[22] Apart from the fact that the distinction between policy and implementation can hardly be applied in practice,[23] it is also unacceptable in principle: the result would have been that no one could have been hold politically responsible for the fraud and mismanagement that took place in the Commission's Departments.

What one can learn here from experiences in the Member States is that at the end of the day a parliament will never accept artificial definitions of political accountability which are introduced by members of the executive and which in fact are aimed at evading accountability. There are good reasons for this.

---

[19] Adam Tomkins, 'Political Accountability in the United Kingdom', in: Luc Verhey, Hansko Broeksteeg and Ilse Van den Driessche (eds.), op. cit., p. 254 ff.

[20] Hansko Broeksteeg, 'Political Accountability in the Netherlands', in: Luc Verhey, Hansko Broeksteeg and Ilse Van den Driessche (eds.), op. cit., p. 165-166.

[21] Jorgen Albaek Jensen, 'Political Accountability in Denmark', in: Luc Verhey, Hansko Broeksteeg and Ilse Van den Driessche (eds.), op. cit., p. 70 ff.

[22] Committee of Independent Experts, Second report on Reform of the Commission, Analysis of current practice and proposals for tackling mismanagement, irregularities and fraud, 10 September 1999, par. 7.9.1 (available on http://www.europarl.eu.int/experts/default_en.htm).

[23] Except perhaps for Sweden. See Joakim Nergelius, 'Political Accountability in Sweden', in: Luc Verhey, Hansko Broeksteeg and Ilse Van den Driessche (eds.), op. cit., p. 233 ff.

Using a restrictive definition, as a result of which no one can be hold to account for failures made within the executive, is unacceptable. This is also true in the European Union. That the European Parliament is not a full-grown parliament, and therefore political accountability differs from the traditional concept in a full-fledged parliamentary system, does not justify a blurred or restricted executive accountability. If we accept that the European Parliament can call the Commission into account, then the Parliament must be able to get a grip on the whole range of its executive activities.

5.4 Collective and Individual Accountability

A third issue is the distinction between collective and individual accountability. There seems to be a consensus in the Member States in so far as collective accountability must result in ministers supporting and defending government's decisions in public even if they personally disagree. The purpose of this is that it enables the parliament and the public to know what the government's position is on a given issue.[24] It implies that individual ministers do not discuss their disagreements in public.

The collective accountability as defined by the Commission so far is unfortunately more restrictive. According to the Commission it would imply that each Commissioner may not call into question a decision taken by the whole Commission and to refrain from disclosing what is said at meetings of the Commission. However, this negative definition seems to be too limited. It enables an individual Commissioner to deny responsibility by saying that a certain decision did not fall within his portfolio, but within that of some other Commissioner.[25]

The Committee of Independent Experts at the time rightly argued a wider approach. Collective accountability also means that commissioners *actively* inform themselves on matters falling within colleagues domains, discuss these matters during the Commission's meetings and *actively* support the Commission's policy once decisions have been made.[26] Unfortunately this critique has not changed the Commission's view at this point. The Prodi Commission published a Code of Conduct for Commissioners in which it replicated the criticized interpretation of collective responsibility articulated by the Santer Commission.[27]

---

[24] Adam Tomkins, op. cit., p. 248 ff.

[25] Critical about this D. Chalmers, C. Hadjiemmanuil, G. Monti and A. Tomkins, *European Union Law*, Cambridge: Cambridge University Press 2006, p. 332: 'Collective responsibility, for the Santer Commission, appeared to revolve around the notion of each Commissioner minding her own business, not rocking the boat, and not querying the work of (or any allegations of wrongdoing) in any other Commissioner'.

[26] Committee of Independent Experts, Second report, op. cit., par. 7.10.2.

[27] This has not changed since then. See Code of Conduct for Commissioners SEC (2004) 1487/2. Principle 1.2. provides: 'Out of respect for the principle of collective responsibility, Commissioners shall not

5.5 A Clear Chain of Command

A fourth recommendation, which could be derived from the common practice in the Member States is: establish a clear chain of command. A precondition for being held accountable is that one has legal powers to implement one's policy. At first sight it seems as if the Commission has the same position as a national government. Much like a national government, the Commission is a collegiate body whose members have their own portfolio. In this context the directorates-general, much like the national ministries, advise the Commissioners on policy matters and are responsible for the sound implementation of the policy decisions of the Commission.

These tasks have been endorsed and worked out in the Code of Conduct of the Commissioners.[28] However, if we look closer, the legal position of the individual Commissioner is unclear. Unlike a national cabinet minister an individual Commissioner is not heading a particular Directorate-General. As a result the portfolios of the Commissioners and the administrative structure are disconnected. There is no clear chain of command that directly links individual Commissioners with the civil service. This leaves individual Commissioners with the situation that they can be held accountable for things happening within their portfolio, but they do not have control over the civil servants who are actually dealing with these matters. This makes the position of a Commissioner rather weak.

As a result the portfolios of the Commissioners and the administrative structure are disconnected. There is no clear chain of command that links individual Commissioners with the civil service. This leaves individual Commissioners with the situation that they can be held accountable for things happening within their portfolio, but they do not have control over the civil servants who are actually dealing with these matters. From an accountability perspective individual Commissioners seem thus to have a weak position.[29]

---

make any comment which would call into question a decision taken by the Commission. They shall also refrain from disclosing what is said at meetings of the Commission'.

[28] SEC (2004) 1487/2. It says, among other things, the following: 'The chain of responsibility continues down to department level in the person of the Director-General, who is answerable to the Commissioner and the College for the proper implementation of the guidelines set by the College and the Commissioner and, in particular, for the management of the Directorate-General or Service in line with the distribution of powers as defined by the Staff Regulations, the Financial Regulation, the Rules of Procedure and the rules laid down as part of the administrative and financial reform of the Commission' (Par. 2.1).

[29] V. Mehde, 'Responsibility and Accountability in the European Commission', *Common Market Law Review* 2003, p. 423 ff.

5.6 Reducing Fragmentation of the Executive

This closely relates to the next practical guideline and which can be summarized by: reduce fragmentation of the executive. In many European countries one can see a growing tendency[30] to cut the executive into smaller pieces. In, for example France, Italy, the Netherlands and the United Kingdom, there has been a haphazard process of establishing a great variety of agencies.[31] In some Member States, like for example France or Italy, this does not seem a serious issue. However, in other Member States agencies have become increasingly controversial. The most important reason for criticizing agencies nowadays is their lack of accountability.

In the Member States there is no consensus on which model of the executive should be enhanced. However, national experiences show that fragmentation of the executive is a serious concern. There is indeed a considerable risk of getting into an obscure system of agencies and policy networks which has become almost inaccessible to the outside world and which are in fact accountable to no one. Here the 'problem of many hands' arises: because many different entities contribute to the decision-making process, it is hard to identify who is, at the end of the day, accountable for the outcome.[32]

The problem of fragmentation seems to raise an important argument in favour of upgrading the Commission as the 'core executive' within the European Union. The great advantage of this would be clarity; one could at least presume that it will then be much clearer for the European Parliament, the Council of Ministers, the European Council, other EU institutions, the Member States and civil society whom one has to call to account for executive decisions of the European Union. The risk of a too powerful, unitary executive at the European level[33] is probably limited because of the comprehensive, multi-level system of checks and balances in which the Commission has to operate.

However, this issue evidently has to be seen in a broader context. The debate about which role the Commission should play in the future is linked with many

---

30 In the traditional model of government a precondition for effective government is the hierarchical structure of the civil service. It enables the parliament to locate accountability at the top of each ministerial department. Traditionally only Sweden has a fundamentally different model: it is based on a constitutional separation between the cabinet and independent administrative agencies. See J. Ziller, 'European Models of Government: Towards a Patchwork with Missing Pieces , *Parliamentary Affairs* 2001, p. 102 ff.

31 See for a comparative research L.F.M. Verhey and T. Zwart (eds.), *Agencies in a comparative and European perspective*, Antwerpen 2003. See also OECD, *Distributed Public Governance. Agencies, authorities and other government bodies*, Paris 2002.

32 M. Bovens, 'Analysing and Assessing Public Accountability: A Conceptual Framework', *European Governance Papers* (EUROGOV), no. C-06-01, 2006, www.connex-network.org/eurogov., p. 18. See also D. Curtin, *Mind the Gap: the Evolving EU Executive and the Constitution*, Third Walter van Gerven Lecture, Leuven Center for a Common Law of Europe, Groningen, Europa Law Publishing 2004, p. 15.

33 See P. Craig, 'The Locus and Accountability of the Executive in the European Union', in: P. Craig and A. Tomkins (eds.), op. cit., p. 344.

other issues than only the accountability of the European executive. One has to take into account the institutional context of the European Union and for example look at the role of other EU institutions, especially the European Parliament, the Council of Ministers and the European Council. Concentrating executive power in the Commission would moreover lead to a diminishing role for the independent agencies. The academic debate on EU agencies shows that that there are several arguments *pro en contra* putting agencies at arms length of the Commission.[34] It has been suggested that clearly identifiable agencies are more visible to the outside world than obscure Commission divisions and therefore contribute to greater transparency and accountability. Leaving open whether this is true or not, it shows that just saying that the Commission should be the 'core executive' in the EU system is not a simple argument to make. However, while debating the future of the EU executive, the risk of fragmentation should be seriously considered.

5.7 Focusing on the Quality of the Account

This brings me to the last lesson we can learn from accountability mechanisms in the Member States: do not focus on resignation, but on the quality of the account. As explained earlier the concept of 'political accountability' in the Member States basically contains three essential elements: being accountable, calling into account and holding to account. In practice it sometimes seems as if politics and public opinion are only interested in the last element. Generally speaking one could say that the process of accountability in the political arena sometimes seems to be reduced to the question of who must get the blame for what has gone wrong. A political climate like this invites ministers to evade their responsibility and to shift the blame to others, particularly to the civil service.

The ultimate sanction of resignation is essential. Without the possibility of sanctions there can be no effective accountability. However, in daily practice accountability is much more than imposing sanctions. It is much more about providing proper information, explaining the cause of events, debating the political issues and trying to determine whether and how the situation should be redressed. One could assume that that is where the public is probably most interested in: trying to find out why things have or have not happened, rectifying possible mistakes and establishing mechanisms to reduce the chance that similar errors would be made in the future.

Seen from this perspective it thus seems more fruitful to invest in the quality of the account than to focus only on resignation. This applies perhaps even more to the European Union. As long as the European Union is no parliamentary system and the European Parliament is no real parliament, there are even fewer reasons to regard resignation of the Commission as the central issue. However, what the European Parliament can do is to try to improve the qual-

[34] E. Vos, 'Reforming the European Commission: What Role to Play for EU Agencies', *CMLRev.* 2000, p. 1113 ff.

ity of the mechanisms by which it calls the Commission and its individual members into account. It could enhance checks and balances within the political system of the European Union and improve the learning capacity and effectiveness of the Commission and its departments and perhaps of other EU institutions as well.

6 Concluding Remarks

This article and the underlying research can be seen as an attempt to formulate some general principles of political accountability. Its scope is limited; it mainly concerns the political accountability of the Commission towards the European Parliament. Other problems of executive accountability, especially the accountability of the Council of Ministers and/or the European Council,[35] are left aside. However, as the fall of the Santer Commission in 1999 and the crisis around the nomination of the Barroso Commission in 2004 have shown, it would be a mistake to neglect or underestimate the importance of the relationship between the Commission and the Parliament. The accountability mechanisms as they exist in this relationship need full attention now and in the future.

Seen from an accountability perspective, there is reason for concern. Writing on a publication on 'Accountability on the EU', Tomkins has concluded that 'it stands as testament to the Prodi Commission's success in effectively closing down the debate on political accountability in the European Union which the reports of the Committee of Independent Experts had seemed, for a short while, to have started'.[36] In the Commission's White Paper on European Governance, and in other documents or proposals, which have been published since, nothing has been said about enhancing the political accountability of the Commission. This is remarkable given the serious fraud and mismanagement, which led to the fall of the Santer Commission in 1999. There is no reason to conclude that a serious debate on political accountability in the European Union is no longer necessary. On the contrary, since 1999, accountability has remained one of the main issues in the debate on European democracy and no real solutions have come up since then.

In trying to clarify what 'political accountability' could mean in the European Union and to improve mechanisms of political accountability, one should take into account the longstanding constitutional traditions in the Member States on this field. Article 6 EU clearly sustains this view: it says that the European Union is founded on the principles of freedom, democracy, human rights and the rule of law principles which 'the Member States have in common.' It would

35 See Olaf Tans, Carla Zoethout, Jit Peters, *National Parliaments and European Democracy. A Bottom-up Approach to European Constitutionalism*, Europa Law Publishing Groningen 2007.

36 D. Chalmers, C. Hadjiemmanuil, G. Monti and A. Tomkins, *European Union Law*, Cambridge: Cambridge University Press 2006, p. 337.

not make sense to look at accountability issues in the European Union while neglecting experiences in the Member States which have been gained in the course of many decades or even centuries. On the contrary, European citizens presumably expect that they will be governed by European institutions that are accountable and that the mechanisms by which European institutions can be held to account are in any case not weaker than the traditional accountability mechanisms at the national level.[37]

Given the foregoing it is important to try to detect which constitutional principles we have in common in Europe and to see if and to what extent the European Union can build upon this 'ius commune' not only to make the European executive more accountable, but also to strengthen the indispensable support of the Member States and its peoples for the decision making process within the European Union. It is self-evident that this cannot take place by simply copying one or more national systems; as repeatedly said before the European Union is not a full-grown parliamentary system and it will not be in the foreseeable future. However, our research has shown that it is worthwhile to have a closer look at national mechanisms of political accountability in order to check more precisely if and how the European Union, in the spirit of article 6 EU, can build upon the longstanding traditions of national constitutionalism.

As said earlier the scope of this article is limited. About these limitations I make two final remarks. The first one regards the question of when and how the general principles of accountability, as described above, should apply. Our starting point was to look at to what extent national accountability mechanisms could be transformed to the relationship between the European Parliament and the Commission. However, problems of accountability are at stake in other relationships as well. Some will say that the problems elsewhere are even more urgent. That is why it would be important to have a closer look at these principles and see if and how they could be applied in other accountability relationships, for example in the relationship between the Parliament and the Council. More research will be needed.

The second remark is about the fact that this article is only about 'political' accountability. This raises a fundamental question: do we still believe in politics? It does not make sense to discuss political accountability if we do not believe that politics should play any role whatsoever. If you don't then you will obviously search for totally different angles and alternative concepts of accountability. This is a crucial issue to keep in mind because it plays a role in all debates on accountability both at the national and at the European level.

---

[37] See further Luc Verhey and Monica Claes, 'Introduction: Political Accountability in an European Perspective', in: Luc Verhey, Hansko Broeksteeg and Ilse Van den Driessche (eds.), op. cit., p. 3 ff.

CHAPTER 6

Political Accountability in Europe

Veith Mehde

As the first discussant, I have got one problem. I regard the findings of the project as very interesting and the conclusions as very plausible. This, of course, makes it slightly difficult to perform the tasks of a discussant. Nevertheless, there is some scope for discussion as far as the normative consequences are concerned. While political scientists are very cautious about drawing conclusions on a normative basis, legal scientists, in my view, have many methodically fully legitimate options to be normative about legal as well as political structures. The reason for the difference between the two sciences might lie in the fact that the law – and especially constitutions or other legal texts that leave room for interpretation – provide a framework of norms that can be further developed and that thereby can be a solid normative basis for further conclusions. In the following, I will first refer to a couple of lessons from the comparative perspective, second I will discuss some aspects of collective and individual responsibility with regard to the members of the Commission and finally, as my last topic, I would like to draw upon the developing culture of accountable government.

I

I think it becomes very clear from the findings of the project that there is a very big difference between the theoretical model – one could also say the legal concept – of political accountability in the various member states, which are described in the country reports, and its political or practical consequences. Also, the theoretical models as such are quite diverse. Nevertheless, in all systems, the public seems to be more or less confident that accountability is at a certain, more or less, satisfactory level. This leads to the question of why this is the case, although the differences in the applied mechanisms seem to suggest that the levels of accountability are far from equal. One possibility could be that the definition of a satisfactory level of accountability has a lot to do with being accustomed to a certain system which one regards as capable of providing the expected results. Historical influences appear to play an important role in developing accountability structures in the respective systems. Obviously, there might be some cases in which the level of accountability suddenly is not regarded as satisfactory any more, especially in case of scandals. Nevertheless, in general terms, the country reports seem to imply that the respective models of accountability that apply in the described political systems are regarded as broadly satisfactory.

This leads to the question of practical or political consequences. It is definitely difficult – even in the aftermath of such a thorough research project – to say if all these national concepts lead to comparable levels of accountability. All we know is that there are very different concepts and we can compare the legal concepts as well as the working mechanisms but there are few hard facts regarding both the quantitative and the qualitative evaluation of the respective models in practice. So, it might well be that there are very coherent, highly developed concepts at a theoretical level, while in practical terms massive dysfunctionalities could be analysed. Generally, it is only in the case of scandals that, in retrospect, one might come to the conclusion that certain chains of command did not work the way they should have worked or accountability mechanisms have not been in place in the way they should have been in place. Consequently, it is also very difficult to say if there is a system in one of the member states that can serve as a model for the whole European Union. It seems impossible to say that one could copy exactly the accountability mechanisms from one of the member states into the European system considering that there is no evidence whatsoever in which way it would actually work in practice.

In this context, it should be taken into account that there are already traditions particular to the European system of decision-making, especially as far as the European Parliament (EP) is concerned. Also, there are already working mechanisms and a certain culture of accountability which seem to be peculiar to the European Parliament. In this context, it should be taken into account that introducing a system, its particular mechanisms, or only certain elements of a certain system into another system might have very different consequences from the ones they have in one of the member states' systems. It is one of the basic rules in the field of comparative law that one should not transfer one element of a legal order into a completely different system and then, at the same time, expect it to have the same consequences in the completely different system. So, it is very difficult to draw any conclusions from there.

A particularly telling example of this fact can be found with regard to accountability as provided by members of Parliament answering questions in public. In the British House of Commons, Parliamentary question time obviously is one of the big events of every parliamentary week. This applies to the most famous Prime Minister's question time, but also to question time of other Cabinet Ministers. Far less known, in the German Bundestag question time also takes place every week – not with the Chancellor appearing before Parliament but with the ministers or other government representatives being obliged to answer questions before Parliament[1]. Quite contrary to the British system, there is virtually no media coverage of this weekly event. It is also a pretty safe guess that if one asked students in the field of law or of political science if there was anything comparable to Minister's question time in Germany, most of them would answer in the negative. So, very similar mechanisms are exercised very differently in two parliamentary systems.

There is especially one conclusion that can be drawn from what was just said about the various systems of accountability. If there is so much difference and if there is not one "normal" level of accountability that applies to all member states, likewise, it becomes unclear what is the standard which gives us an idea of the appropriate and democratically acceptable level of accountabil-

---

1 http://www.bundestag.de/wissen/glossar/f/fragestunde.html (last visited 12th March 2009).

ity. Under these circumstances, it seems even more difficult to determine the democratic deficit in the European Union as far as accountability is concerned. Paradoxically, the more one knows about different systems of accountability and therefore about different levels of democratic legitimacy, the less clear-cut the benchmarks seem to become.

II

One of the very specific features of the European system has been the traditional importance of the collective accountability of the Commissioners. The gradual expansion of a structure of individual accountability is probably one of the most interesting developments in the institutional structure within the European treaties: the Commission started off as a collective body with no individual responsibility of any kind in place and with no formal position of the President of the Commission. Basically, in the founding treaties, the Commission was designed as a uniform political actor. Commissioners had no significant role of their own. Their role was almost exclusively to be a member of the Commission. Nowadays, the particular successful elements of the work of the Commission could well be said to be based on very strong Commissioners. The Commission has developed a culture of individual accountability, at least as far as the in the public Commissioners are expected to be accountable for what is going on in their portfolio. Also, the President of the Commission is in a much stronger legal position. So from the historical perspective, the Commission has developed much more towards a governmental position as part of a parliamentary system. The developments that can be witnessed from the changes in the rules set out by the treaties point towards the advance of a "normal" parliamentary system.

The structure of the Commission will change again, especially once the Lisboan treaty comes into force. In particular, there will not be one Commissioner from each member state any longer. The whole idea of collective responsibility, of creating a collective body in which the national affiliations of the Commissioners don't feature prominently, of having only the collective body that is actually there to represent collectively the interest of the whole Union – all this might be fading away once the governments of the member states do not have "their" Commissioner who they can regard as "their" representative. This might lead to a situation where one looks much more closely at the individual Commissioner and his or her decisions – irrespective of their national origin. The focus, in other words, might be more on the subject matters Commissioners are dealing with and less on their national background.

In this situation, it must be regarded as an even worse conceptual mismatch not to make the Commissioners the formal heads of their departments or "their" Directorates General (DG). At the moment, all that is known in this respect is that the head of the DG is the Director General. Also, one knows which subject matter each Commissioner is responsible for. At the same time, not each Commissioner has one DG within his or her portfolio. So there is a conceptual mismatch that cannot really be solved without formalising the system so that the Commissioner actually is the head of a DG or another administrative body he or she is responsible for. This seems to be one of the conclusions that should be drawn from the developments that have taken place so far and that will also be going on in the near future.

III

So, all one can say after these conclusions is that one should hope for a satisfying level of accountability being in place in the European political system. It is very difficult to actually say what are the corner stones characterising such a level. Just like in the member states, the various actors involved in the political system of the EU have to keep developing a culture that can be regarded as satisfactory and as appropriate for the subject matters the Commission is dealing with. Obviously, all this takes place in an extremely and increasingly complex government structure. It seems that the Commission has realised that there is a problem of fragmentation and that everything should be avoided that could make the whole political and administrative structure even more complex and less transparent. So, fragmentation and the complex government structure are certainly something that should be reviewed and it seems that a process might be starting in that respect.

It becomes very clear from the comparative research that the key element in the process of holding to account certainly is the EP, but also the respective parliaments in the member states. Obviously, at a European level, there is only the EP that can fulfil the same function as national parliaments in the member states. At the same time, national parliaments must also be involved in the process of decision-making in the EU, and national parliaments should have all the instruments to make sure that accountability standards are actually applied. So the question is how to get to a coherent framework for both the EU and the member states as far as their role in the process of European decision-making is concerned.

In this context, the legal scrutiny by the ECJ should also be regarded as a topic in the context of the debate about political accountability. It seems wrong to talk about political accountability more or less as opposed to legal questions. In many respects, the ECJ always has been a political actor involved in the process of integration and perhaps one should follow that tradition also in this respect. While there has been a heated discussion about the active role the ECJ played in developing the Union and in furthering integration, the Court might play an active role also in furthering and increasing accountability structures. In this respect, the ECJ could be the institution to help the MEPs to get their accountability standards put in place. Generally, with regard to accountability, resignation or even punishment of officials is a topic. In this sense, it would certainly be felt as a sanction if the ECJ were to say that the Commission had failed in properly giving account to the EP. In other words, one should see the political potential that these legal instruments actually have. The European Communities and the European Union have always been examples of a legalistic form of integration. The administration in the European Union still is very small compared to the administrations in the member states. Consequently, the EU is an institution based on legalistic or legal integration. So why not try to actually implement legal rules that make it possible for the ECJ to scrutinise very effectively the accountability structures?

CHAPTER 7

The European Commission and Parliamentary Oversight

Michael Shackleton

The discussion of political accountability at the European level prompts three questions from my perspective as a practitioner from inside the EU institutions:

- first, can we compare the European Parliament with national parliaments in developing accountability?
- second, should we focus our attention on the European Commission as the "core executive" to be held to account?, and
- third, does the EU system of checks and balances ensure adequate accountability in terms of transparency?

In addressing the first question, it seems to me to be unhelpful to compare the European Parliament with the national parliaments in the Member States of the European Union. Such a comparison quickly leads to the suggestion that the accountability conundrum can be addressed by making the European Commission responsible to a parliamentary majority. To pursue such a logic is to propose a *fusion of powers* with the legislature the ultimate arbiter of the fate of the executive.

In practice, the Parliament has developed its most significant powers on the basis of a very different logic. On a cumulative basis since the Maastricht Treaty it has acquired a significant level of legislative power but a power that is shared with the Council of Ministers under the codecision procedure (known as the "ordinary legislative procedure" under the Lisbon Treaty).

The logic of this procedure is much more akin to the idea of a *separation of powers*, with Commission, Parliament and Council, each institution enjoying legally enshrined autonomous rights, with none subjugated to the will of either of the other two.

In such a system, the European Parliament is much more likely to develop into something akin to the House of Representatives than to become a European level House of Commons, National Assembly or Bundestag.

It can be argued that the Parliament's power of appointment and dismissal of the Commission contradicts such a notion of a separation of powers. However, the right of censure is much more akin to the power of the United States Congress to impeach the President than to the power of a parliamentary majority to withdraw support, all the more so given the lack of any such stable majority within the institution. And the right of approval of the Commission – even as amended in the Lisbon Treaty – remains a power that is shared with the European Council: it is not a power that the Parliament can exercise on its own.

The European Union is based on the idea of balance of power between institutions with none able to control the others directly. Indeed the force of this claim can be measured by considering the impact of the Parliament having the right to appoint the Commission on its own. Under a parliamentary system of such a kind, the executive would presumably have the right of dissolution of the Parliament. Such an idea was discussed in the course of the proceedings of the Convention but no one seriously wished to follow such a route.

As in the United States, there is a strong desire to avoid the centralisation of power, despite the losses in efficiency that the existing system can generate. As Magnette has written, "the pyramidal and hierarchical structure of the parliamentary state is replaced by horizontal relations of mutual control".[1] The answer to the problem of accountability has to take account of this structure.

As for the second question, namely whether the Commission is the "core executive", here too I have my doubts. It might be comforting to suppose that we should establish straight lines of accountability linked to the central position of the Commission but there is much evidence to suggest that we are moving away from such a notion and indeed that the Member States collectively have no desire to clarify the relations of responsibility in this way.

Any assessment of the executive function at EU level is bound to come to the conclusion that responsibility is becoming increasingly diffused as the number of executive bodies proliferates. Rather than underlining the central role of the Commission, the Member States have preferred to create additional institutions to take on executive tasks. It is not the Commission that will coordinate the work of the European Council but rather a newly created President, whose precise tasks remain to be defined but who will surely come to play an important part in the executive structure of the EU. She or he will, of course, be subject to no direct control in terms of appointment or dismissal by the European Parliament.

Even within the existing structures, we can see how the logic of the institutions does not point to the Commission as a "core executive" body. If we were moving towards a parliamentary regime, we would expect the Parliament to become the body through which the executive passed its proposal for any piece of new legislation. In fact, in the EU system, the Commission does enjoy the right of initiative but effectively loses ownership of a proposal in the course of the legislative procedure. At the end of that procedure, it is Council and Parliament that can be (and often are) taken to the European Court of Justice for the law that they enact. The Commission simply does not enjoy a position that could be defined as that of a "core executive".

Does the EU system of checks and balances do enough to ensure accountability, particularly in relation to transparency? There must be considerable doubts: the process of decision-making raises important questions as to the quality of the accountability that can be effectively exercised.

The most obvious indicator of the lack of transparency relates to the tendency for Council and Parliament increasingly to come to agreement in codecision at first reading, very rarely now proceeding to the final stage of conciliation. The impact of this change, whether sought or not by the institutions themselves, is one that significantly raises the barriers to accountability:

- first, it is very difficult to identify the sources of changes to Commission proposals, in the way that is much easier to do when agreements are reached later in the procedure;

1 Quoted in Shackleton, M. (2005), 'Parliamentary Government of Division of Powers: Is the Destination Still Unknown?', in: C. Parsons and N. Jabko (eds) *The State of the European Union: With US or Against US* (Oxford and New York: Oxford University Press), p. 132.

- second, it is very hard to know who is negotiating on behalf of the Council and Parliament, in notable contrast with conciliation where strict rules of participation have been laid down: and
- third, the opportunities for interested parties from outside the institutions to become involved are significantly reduced as they are effectively presented with a "fait accompli", negotiated by a small group and only requiring a simple majority in the Parliament (whereas second reading amendments require an absolute majority).

Accountability in its fullest sense requires the broadest political debate, involving national parties and parliaments as well as those closer to the action in Brussels. This does not mean that the procedure should allow those not directly involved to block indefinitely – in any case, this is impossible once a common position is adopted and the deadlines of the treaty take effect. EU decision-makers need to be allowed to act responsibly for those issues within their competence. And yet the procedures must be ones that all can have confidence in and believe offer an adequate opportunity to identify how a decision was taken and by whom. Present arrangements do not guarantee this.

CHAPTER 8

National Parliaments and Political Accountability in Europe

Jan Jacob van Dijk

First of all, I would like to congratulate the editors of, and contributors to, the edited volume on political accountability in Europe.[1] The book provides a good overview of how political accountability in national parliaments is taking place, and I think that it is a very good initiative to bring out literature about the situation in other EU Member States, which everybody can understand, and from which everybody can learn. However, allow me also to make a few critical remarks.

Do we still believe in politics? That was one of the questions Luc Verhey put forward in his address. And, my question is: what kind of politics? When I am talking with people in the street, they have a completely different interpretation of politics than I have, being a politician in the national parliament. When we, in the Dutch parliament, recently considered reforms to our education system, one of the first questions journalists raised was: who should take the blame? That is not the way I see politics – I believe politics are about organising things to improve the life of citizens in society. But, from the point of view of the general public, politics seem to be more of a kind of entertainment, e.g. who might be forced to resign next?

My second remark concerns the role of the national parliament itself. Historically, the national parliament occupied itself with national policy, national politics, and with what the national government could do both domestically and internationally. Quite often, the national parliament dealt with international aspects of policies only at a moment when there was an international treaty, which had to be ratified. At that moment, of course, the only question before parliament was: do we, or do we not, accept the treaty. There would be no possibility of changing it, or of issuing additional demands to the national government for further negotiations. Perhaps there are historical exceptions, but in general, this was the situation. The situation completely changed at the moment that supranational organisations were installed. In that respect, the European Commission and the Council of Ministers made it difficult for national parliamentarians to choose what kind of role they would like to play. They could either extend their role as national politicians, overseeing national government officials as they did in a domestic context, threatening the government with forced resignation if it failed to reach a certain desired result. Alternatively, they could adopt the role associated with the context of international politics, whereby parliamentarians could merely issue an opinion in the hope that the government would do its best to have it implemented and report back. So, what kind of role should a national parliament play in European affairs?

In the Dutch parliament, we in fact observe three different situations. The first one concerns the General Affairs Council covering external relations and, to a certain extent, the European Council. Here the setting corresponds to the situation of classical international politics. Parliamentarians might send a

[1] L. Verhey, H. Broeksteeg and I. Van den Driessche, eds, *Political Accountability in Europe: Which Way Forward? A Traditional Concept of Parliamentary Democracy in an EU Context*, Groningen: Europa Law Publishing 2008.

message to the government regarding desired results, yet a threat of a forced resignation or no-confidence vote over the issue would not be an option. The opposite is the case with respect to the Justice and Home Affairs Council. When the Third Pillar was introduced as part of the European Union by the Maastricht Treaty, no substantive role was provided for the European Parliament; in response to that, the Netherlands introduced a new kind of instrument whereby Dutch approval to a decision in the Council could only be given by the competent minister after prior approval from the Dutch parliament. In a 'normal' situation, however, such as regarding the Council configurations on competitiveness, social policy, environment etc., there still is confusion about the exact role of the national parliament. Should the Dutch parliament itself be participating in the European legislative process; should it focus on seeking to enforce accountability of the Dutch government for conduct within European negotiations; should we perhaps establish a procedure along the lines of the Danish mandate system, or expand the existing prior-assent procedure with respect to the Third Pillar across the board? The discussion is in fact restarting again as some people argue that the role of the national parliaments should be more active than it is at this moment. I myself have strong reservations against focusing too much on mandating routines. If members of parliament wish to have any real influence – which might be different from enforcing accountability – it is imperative that they start as early as possible in the legislative process. If they were to wait until the end of the negotiations and intervene just before the final decision, then their possible impact is limited to changing a sentence or two.

My third remark concerns the role of European agencies, as also mentioned by Luc Verhey in his contribution. At the moment, at the national level but certainly at the European level, there is much doubt as to whether European agencies are desirable, and whether we need to establish more of them. From an accountability perspective, and in the context of the role of national parliaments, European agencies are highly problematic. However, when opposing the creation of new agencies in practice, we do not always enjoy sufficient support from other national parliaments or the European Parliament. This makes the task of containing the proliferation of European agencies extremely difficult.

My fourth remark concerns COSAC, and whether we need more inter-parliamentary meetings within COSAC. My answer to this question is no, we do not need more meetings. There are national parliamentarians who would like to have more meetings, assuming that more meetings will translate into greater influence for national parliaments. However, my own view is that the higher the meeting frequency, the more the exercise will degenerate into parliamentary tourism, and the less influence parliamentarians will end up having. There are new ways, new instruments by which influence and accountability processes can be organized. What is really of the essence is inter-parliamentary cooperation on issues such as subsidiarity and proportionality. Those are aspects in which national parliaments have to play a more important role, and on which they have to cooperate more with each other.

The fifth and final observation I would like to submit concerns the notion that the European Commission is the core institution on which to focus accountability processes. There is one aspect that, in my view, deserves more attention, which is the role of comitology. We know that there are a great number of executive committees in which officials from national governments and the European Commission are taking decisions together. In what way can we extract a degree of accountability from them as well? Here national parliaments are at a disadvantage because, at the moment, they lack information about what is happening there.

Thus, we should always be aware that accountability enforcement in national parliaments for European policy-making is fundamentally different from domestic accountability processes, and that accountability for comitology is a crucial element in the larger complex of accountability for European policy-making. More generally speaking, the democratic deficit at the European level has in my view not so much to do with the role of the European Parliament. It has to do with a dysfunctional control by national parliaments over the European Council of Ministers and the European Council. There are several aspects in which national parliaments should play a more active role than they do now.

CHAPTER 9

Politicians, Bureaucrats and the Reinvention of the European Commission

From Technical to "Good Governance"

Anchrit Wille

1 Introduction

For many people, the Commission has become associated with a dysfunctional politicized bureaucracy being permeated by national interests. Over the past ten years the European Commission has, however, undergone its most significant internal changes since its inception. A range of internal administrative reform measures aimed to create a completely modernised public international administration based on the principles of accountability, transparency and efficiency. The resignation of the Santer Commission in 1999 following the accusations of mismanagement, irregularities and fraud was one of the impetuses for this internal reform. The achievement of the EU's largest and most complex enlargement in May 2004 – the European Union was to include 10+2 new Member States – was an additional incentive. These reforms, in combination with revisions from the treaties of Maastricht, Amsterdam and Nice altering the Commission's legal and political framework, have affected the Commission's executive responsibilities, the operation of its college of commissioners and its administration. New structures and rules with a range of ex ante constraints and ex post incentives combined to provide a system for more control and accountability in and over a 'reinvented' Commission (Peterson 2006). The reforms are generally perceived as the most radical internal modernization since the Commission was established fifty years ago in 1958.

In this paper I will map the modernization of the Commission. I will show how changes in the in the past decade – during the Prodi (1999-2004) and Barroso (2004-2009) tenures – have *strengthened the basic architecture of political control and accountability* in the European Commission. I will try to reflect on how these shifts in political control and accountability have put new political pressures and demands on the working of the Commission in terms of its political executive function and its bureaucracy; and what the reforms have meant in terms of *political and professional roles.*

2 The Commission: Technocratic Politicians and Politicized Bureaucrats

Many have long viewed the Commission as a *technocratic and impartial body*. This harks back to the origins of the European project and the legacy of Jean Monnet, which bestowed a particular conception that a politicized EU would contain winners and losers and this could undermine rather than reinforce the legitimacy of the EU. The High Authority of the European Coal and Steel Community (and its institutional successor the Commission) was meant to provide the impetus for integration ('motor of integration') and to be the guardian of the common European interest. Decisions about how these interests were to be specified and pursued, could better not be subject to some kind of democratic 'majoritarian' mechanism. The integration and mediating function should be guided by the judgement of a technocratic elite rather than by political judgement. Politicians bound to be short-sighted and self-seeking, as they are subject to electoral mechanisms. It would make for better governance to take the impartial, the overall and long term view of the technocrat. Successful integration required consensus about practical goals and abstinence from power politics, hard political choices and conflict (Hooghe & Marks 2005). The Commission's role as a guardian of the European interest would depend on its expertise and its credibility as an independent mediator between political views, conflicting national interests and interest group pressures. In the original design of the European Commission politics was therefore 'organized out'.

The image of the Commission as a technocratic institution contrasts with a different image, that of the Commission as *a 'politicized' bureaucracy* (Christiansen 1997, Peterson 2008). Formally, the Commission possessed many of the classic characteristics of a textbook case of a Weberian hierarchical organization (Page 1997; Hooghe 2001: 200). But in the practice of the EU system, the Commission, was less bureaucratic than other bureaus. Policymaking in the EU is not only subject to the extensive bargaining and deliberation in the legislative phase, but policies are also bound to be renegotiated when it comes to their implementation in different national contexts. As Christiansen (1997: 77) argued: 'having to manage the resultant clash between pervasive political interests and the rigidities of the *acquis communautaire* is what makes the Commission such a special type of public administration'.

In addition, the educational, professional and cultural background of top-officials was extra-ordinarily divers and far more heterogeneous than that of top-officials in any national bureaucracy. Country of origin was highly important and the first meaning of the adjective political in the European circles was 'nationality'. Studies in the mid 90s showed that national identifications in the Commission were important for network-building and sometimes became institutionalized in units, divisions and even whole DGs (Egeberg, 1996; Christiansen 1997). Promotions at the top of the Commission depended on one's nationality and support from one's national government – not on merit or loyalty to the Commission hierarchy. In the past, senior officials in the Commission were often 'parachuted' in from national administrations – and there was an informal system of 'flagging' where certain director-general posts were expected to be held by nationals of particular countries. For many years, nationality represented at the same time a condition and a limit to the accession to posts of directors-general (Georgakakis & de Lasalle 2007: 6). Moreover, the large number of seconded national experts has often been considered as fulfilling a national 'meddling' role in the Commission (Trondal 2004). National quotas and temporary contracts have 'politicized' the Commission bureaucracy. The fact that the Commission is a multinational bureaucracy had a fundamental impact on its cohesion, demographic character and the form of political control (Page 1997, Hooghe 2001). Failures to meld different cultures, of which the Commission bureaucracy is composed and which have proved hard to unify, long time impeded the internal cohesion of the Commission bureaucracy (Harlow 2002: 59-60).

Several structural conditions have, in addition, politicized and fragmented the Commission (Christiansen 1997). A lack of integration between the political – the commissioners – and the bureaucratic level – DG's – was one of the main 'political control' problems in the Commission (CIE 1999). Cabinets that constituted a link between the bureaucratic and the political Commission often interfered in the work of the DG's in the past and contributed to a widened gap between the political and the bureaucratic level. Moreover, the inter-departmental conflicts and competitions – manifested itself in bureaucratic politics and turf wars – were another expression of politicization in the Commission bureaucracy. Finally, the network of thousand of committees of national and Commission officials – called comitology – with real influence in the making of European policy also played a part in the politicized nature of the Commission.

The upshot of this all was that the line between politics and technocracy was far from clear in the Commission and was constantly blurred by the behaviour of many officials (Fouilleux a.o 2005). In the words of Hooghe (2001: 7): 'in the complex setting of the European Union, Commission officials often find it impossible to resolve the tension between politics and expertise and impartiality'.

3 Reforming the European Commission

During the mid nineties it was, clear that the Commission was experiencing serious *political, management and credibility* problems.

A first problem concerns the gradual erosion of the legitimacy of the EU and the Commission in particular. This process of legitimacy loss started already in the context of the discussion that preceded the Maastricht Treaty of 1992. The legitimacy of the EU integration process, its governance and its institutions came under fire (Tsakatika 2005: 200-204). Europe was charged with a 'democratic deficit' which weighed heavily on its legitimate *governance*. One of the critical assessments was that an independent and unaccountable technocratic elite in the Commission was allowed to become so powerful. Consequently, the EU has been involved, since the early 1990s, in the preparation, the negotiation or the ratification of a *treaty reform* every few year by Member States in intergovernmental conferences (IGCs). The long series of treaty revision – Maastricht, Amsterdam, Nice – had to change the legal and political framework governing the appointment and tasks of the Commission in order to change it into an effectively accountable institution.

For some the real problem with European *governance* was not the Commission's traditionally weak democratic credentials (input legitimacy) but its diminishing problem solving efficiency (output legitimacy). The Commission's organization came under increasing attack in the mid 1990s for handling of its executive responsibilities. The organization had, as Peterson (2006) calls it, 'plumbing problems': it tended to leak money and work inefficiently. Over the 1990s, as the pace of the European integration picked up, the size of the Union increased and its range of policies expanded, the Commission suffered the consequences of success. The assignment of an ever-increasing range of tasks and responsibilities (Christiansen 2001: 758) diluted the Commission's core commitments' (Majone 2002: 389). As a response to these problems, the Santer commission launched several reform initiatives, in order to improve executive performance (Nugent 2001: 177). The Commission was, however, not particularly receptive to new management ideas and has known a long history of failure to reform (Cini 2000; Stevens and Stevens 2006). Santer was unable to win support for his reform initiatives in the ranks of the Commission and incapable to change the culture of the organization (Cini 2000).

The result has not only been a weakening of the organization but also a loss of its trust. The Commission lost much of its authority it enjoyed under Delors. Weak leadership and ineffective management have eroded its standing vis-à-vis other EU institutions. Dissatisfaction with of the way the Commission functioned, especially among the largest and more powerful EU member governments, meant that none of the big players were prepared to spend political capital defending the Commission (Peterson 2004: 15). Lack of support in major capitals contributed to a political marginalisation of the Commission. In fact, the larger states, led alternately by France, the UK and Germany have frequently been keen to clip the Commissioner's wings (Spence 2006: 26); and many national leaders were less than enthusiastic about entrusting it with new powers, preferring to co-operate among themselves on issues they consider to be at the core of national sovereignty.

Fraud allegations and corruption scandals then tarnished its reputation. One may debate whether it was 'chance' or an 'accident waiting to happen' (Pollitt and Bouckaert 2004: 234), but the series of scandals and inefficiencies that surrounded the Commission at the end of the nineties left its mark. The resignation of the Santer Commission in March 1999 following accusations of mismanagement, irregularities and fraud, pushed reform to the top of the political agenda of the Commission.

Prodi, Santer's successor as Commission President, was accordingly appointed very much on the basis of a mandate to reform the Commission and to restore confidence in the organization. It is against this background of crisis and discussion about the problematic political legitimacy of European Commission, that the newly appointed Commission was coming with strategy to regain its threatened credibility. In July 2001, the European Commission issued a *White Paper on European Governance*, which announced a range of internal reform measures that would transform the functioning and administration of the Commission and its executive responsibilities. The evolution of the Commission had to be seen in the broader perspective of '*principles of good governance*' identified in the White Paper as *openness, participation, accountability, effectiveness and coherence.*

Following this *White Paper*, the Commission and its staff have been engaged in the task of overhauling administrative systems and procedures to equip the institution with a modern, efficient and effective European civil service These reforms, in combination with revisions from the treaties altering the Commission's legal and political framework, have affected the Commission's executive responsibilities, the operation of its college of commissioners and its administration.

4 The College of Commissioners: the Evolution to a Political Executive

'Parliamentarization': towards a 'grown' executive-legislative relationship

Since the rise of the deficit narrative at the beginning of the 1990s the European Parliament (EP) in particular has gained considerable powers and influence in the EU policy-making process. With every treaty change in the past years the EP has successfully managed to extend its powers and also the accountability of the Commission to the Parliament. The Maastricht treaty (1992) marks the beginning of Parliament's metamorphosis into the role of co-legislator by introducing full legislative power ('co-decision') in certain policy areas, and by extending the co-operation procedure to others.[1]

In a 1999 resolution the EP advocated a strong link between the preferences expressed by Union citizens in EP elections and the nomination of the College of Commissioners and its programme for the parliamentary term. Consequently, the term of office of Colleges has been extended from four to five years so as to bring them into close alignment with the term of the EP elections. The EP has gradually gained more weight in the appointment procedure claiming not only the right to be consulted on the choice of the President but also the right to approve his appointment. Steps have been taken to render the College directly accountable to the EP as illustrated by the EP committees' examination of nominated Commissioners, its vote of confidence, and its right to dismiss the entire College. These new initiatives have brought the EU rather close to a parliamentary system (Judge and Earnshaw 2002; Van Gerven 2007).

The new investiture procedures by the EP may contribute to a new form of 'credit' that commissioners can build up for their internal and external leadership during their mandate; commissioners can claim to represent a legitimacy

1 The Maastricht Treaty brought the term of office of the Commission into line with the term of the European Parliament and gave parliament the power of final approval over the membership of the Commission. The Amsterdam Treaty (1997) extended co-decision to most areas of legislation, and reformed the procedure to put the Parliament on an equal footing with the Council. The Nice Treaty (2000) extended co-decision to seven more areas. As a result of this successive increase in power, the EP has extended its position in legislative co-decision-making, its budgetary powers are very considerable and its powers of control and over EU appointments have been reinforced.

which is not simply based upon bureaucratic hierarchical rank but reflects the facts that their appointment is a political one – supported by the EP-procedure. Enhanced parliamentary accountability arrangements had important consequences for the political role of commissioners. Being held accountable by MEPs, today's commissioners are required to defend and justify the decisions and actions falling within their sphere of competence.

Judge and Earnshaw (2002) point out that *parliamentarization* has made the relationship between the Commission and the EP becomes increasingly confrontational. The EP's role in the Commission crisis of the Santer Commission in 1999 and the appointment of the Barrosso Commission at the end of 2004 are only the most dramatic manifestation of this changed relationship (Cram 2002). In face of opposition within the Parliament to several nominees, President-designate Barroso, was led to ask for a postponement of the Parliament's scheduled vote of approval and consequently to modify his proposed College of Commissioners. The European Parliament gave finally its endorsement to the Commission line-up after José Manual Barroso, the new Commission President, had agreed to drop two of the original nominees and to reshuffle two other portfolios after a storm of protests from parliament. The formal approval of the European Parliament ended a looming institutional showdown. The episode is just one of the illustrations how the Commission has gradually evolved into an institution that must pay far greater attention to politics than it did in the past. The new 731-member EP wanted to show that it is a force to be reckoned with. The incident was an indication of the power struggle between the three main EU institutions, the EP, the Commission and the Council.

All this inevitably has contributed a greater political control over the Commission. With the treaty reforms a range of ex ante incentives and ex post constraints are introduced that may entail a stronger role in the daily policy-making and closer contact between the Commission and Parliament (in areas of co-decision). The European Parliament has become a far more vociferous and demanding interlocutor and this may have contributed to the design of a more politically accountable Commission: 'the certainties of the essentially technocratic relationship into which the Commission has bound itself may now be giving way to a more politicised relationship' (Westlake 2006: 277).

Presidentialization and 'ministerialism'

One other mechanism that has contributed to enhanced political control over the Commission is the role of the President. His role until the Amsterdam Treaty was little more than that of 'first among equals', but over time his powers has been steadily grown in importance. Today it seems accepted that the work of the College of commissioners shall be subject to his political leadership. The President has got the power to decide on the internal organization of the Commission and to allocate the responsibilities of the commissioners both at the time of appointment and throughout the term of the Commission (Christiansen 2001: 754). The Amsterdam Treaty increased the powers of the president over his fellow commissioners by allowing him to decide who does which portfolio and to reshuffle them during their five year term of office; he even can request an individual commissioner to resign. Due to the principle of collegiality – the College has to approve the President's request for the resignation of commissioners, but the new powers of the President should strengthen his role vis-à-vis the individual Commissioners and allows him in principle to run the Commission with greater authority. These developments can be read as a form of top-down politicization of the college; it is an attempt to make the commissioners more responsible for their portfolios and in overseeing their services; and should they fail to perform, they can be sanctioned by the President (Christiansen 2001: 754). The enhanced presidential authority should also make it easier to co-ordinate the many tasks of the Commission and to ensure that it pulls in one direction.

Prodi was the first incumbent to enjoy the enhanced powers (introduced under the Amsterdam Treaty) granted to the office as part of the reforms (Dimitrakopoulos & Kassim 2005: 187). Prodi's conception of how the Commission should operate has given shape to elements of, what Peterson (2004) calls, both *Presidentialism* and *Ministerialism* which have affected its executive role. Prodi was the first former Prime Minister of a large country to be appointed Commission President and his conception of the Commission led him to organize its structures on governmental lines. Prodi decided not to retain a portfolio for himself, which enabled him 'to present himself as the political figurehead at the top of the Commission' (Peterson 2004: 17). Barroso continued this 'presidential' role by stating at the start of his new Commission that he intends to adopt a more hands-on approach to managing the Commission than his predecessors to ensure all the commissioners work together effectively.

The growing ministerial background of commissioners, a significant trend which manifested itself since the first Commission (Macmullen 2000: 46), indicates a move away from technical towards a political approach. An analysis of Commissioners' prior jobs in the political arena shows that Member States now rely extensively around 79% on candidates with high political visibility turning the college into an increasingly political body (Wonka 2007).

(Party) Political profile

To the extent that the Commission becomes less a body of technocrats and more a political body, we should start looking for instances where Commissioners assume party-political roles as well. Although the party political role is the least frequently evoked role at College meetings, Egeberg (2006a) expects that party politicization of the college of commissioners will in some situations complement or even displace cleavages along sectoral and national lines.

Barroso is a member of the European People's Party and was appointed by the European Council in June 2004 in response to the victory of the EPP-ED in the 2004 European elections. This was the first time the Commission President had been appointed according to the results of the latest European Elections. With the Barroso Commission the political centre-of-gravity changed and became more right-wing than the previous two Commissions; both the Prodi and the Santer Commissions contained narrow left of centre majorities. This shifting political balance is not simply a function of the changing color of the Member State governments in the Council. An important reason, according to Hix (2004, 2006) is that the Barroso Commission was the first to be appointed whereby each Member State has only one Commissioner. Hix argues that when this change in the structure of representation in the Commission is combined with the introduction of qualified-majority voting for electing the Commissioner President, the prospect is a significantly more partisan Commission: the Commission President can be elected by a smaller political majority, and he will then be able to lead a Commission where his political allies are likely to be in majority.

In previous years, the Commission and its commissioners tended to keep a distance between Brussels and national politics, hovering somewhat above the domestic fray. Yet under the Prodi and Barroso leadership commissioners appear to cultivate more explicit political roles. The revised Code of Conduct for commissioners allows them to be active members of political parties or trade unions. If they are to play an active role in an election campaign they have to 'withdraw from the work of the Commission for the duration of the campaign Louis Michel, the EU's commissioner for development, took on unpaid leave to campaing in Belgium's federal elections. Margot Wallstrom, the EU communications commissioner, made an all-out plug for French socialist president candidate Segolene Royal in her blog. Dutch commissioner Neelie Kroes openly supported Angela Merkel to become chancellor just days before the German elections. During the last Commission Italian prime minister Romano Prodi actively campaigned in the general elections in Italy while still head of the Brussels executive and Greek commissioner Anna Diamantopoulou also took a leave of absence for domestic elections and then resigned after winning a seat.

During the Barroso tenure three Commissioners left to fulfil high profile posts back home. Markos Kyprianou, EU health commissioner, resigned March 2008 from his job to become foreign minister of Cyprus following the election of a new Cypriot president. Later Italian commissioner Franco Frattini, who was in charge of the important justice and home affairs portfolio, followed him. And in October 2008 European Union trade commissioner Peter Mandelson left his position with the EU's executive and took up the position of secretary of state for business in UK Prime Minister Gordon Brown's cabinet. These reshufflings in the College is indicative for the political profile of today's commissioners.

Responsiveness to the Citizen's Agenda

The Commission's public communication suffered a long time from the fragmentation of political authority, a pervasive technocratic mindset and a lack of adequate staffing. The transformation process European governance was undergoing turned media communication progressively relevant to the survival of the European Commission. At the start of the new period Barroso, repeatedly emphasized his desire tot improve the Commission's communication record. Looking back over the last decade one can find numerous calls to 'reconnect with the citizens'. Communication commissioner Wallström presented *plan D* (in 2005), followed by the *White Paper on a European Communication Policy* (presented in May 2006) which is meant to narrow the communication gap looming between the European Union and its citizens and to map a way towards the development of European public sphere.

The launched proposals in Plan D – for Democracy, Dialogue and Debate – build on various initiatives taken during the *'pause for reflection'* that followed the negative French and Dutch referenda in 2005. They propose a wide variety of opportunities for European citizens to become involved in debate and discussion – preferably transnational. The internet facilitates such opportunities through websites, blogs, e-polling, discussion forums and the rest. All promoted through an intensive communications strategy. In the words of the Communications Commissioner, Margot Wallstrom: 'to regain the confidence of the public, the Commission will harness all its resources, both internally and externally, to deliver solutions to the issues raised by citizens. This is a policy response centred around a citizens' agenda'. 'European democracy,' she said, 'And European communications policy is not about getting the people on board. It's about putting them in the driving seat'. These activities in the direction of the public can be interpreted as a form of increased *responsive* to the interests of the European public, as if it were a representative body of the people serving the collective interests of the European polity.

5 Administrative Reforms: Depoliticizing to Control

The increased emphasis on the individual responsibility of Commissioners for the administrative services within their respective portfolios introduced the need for some structural changes in the Commission. Confronted with retaining the political responsibility for what happens in their portfolio, commissioners are in need of controlling an apparatus that is more professional and less politicized. The programme of Commission reform being announced by the Prodi Commission in March 2000 contained several measures.

Modernization of the Commission's bureaucracy

In March 2000 the new commissioner in charge of reforms Kinnock announced a set of proposals in a Reform Strategy White Paper for what he called a 'root, branch, trunk and trees' reform of the institution (Kassim 2004). Changes entailed: a) modernization of the complete system of financial management and control; b) the introduction of more efficient and performance-oriented working methods such as *'Strategic Planning and Programming'* to achieve a more efficient and transparent annual focus on the main operational priorities and their operational consequences; c) a modernization of personnel policy by a new Human Resources Strategy.

A programme of departmental mergers reduced the number of directorates-general from 42 to 35 in order to increase political control and improve the policy-making coherence. Moreover, Prodi directed that directors-general should be rotated to new posts periodically and could not share the same nationality as the Commissioner responsible for their service (Peterson 2004: 26). This re-shuffling of director-generals may ensure that permanent officials don't dominate their Commissioners

The overwhelming proportion of measures proposed by the White Paper has been implemented in a very short space of time. The reform programme intended to monitor its employees' actions more accurately, and to bring preferences in line with its ambitions for control. The main thrust was to strengthen control and to increase the quality of strategic decision-making. The reforms were an attempt to 'depoliticize' the Commission bureaucracy from a number of political – read 'national' – influences. The idea was to detach the organization from responsiveness to national interest and to move away from practices with national quotas. Though the national balance principle has not been completely removed from appointments and promotions criteria, it is clearly being downgraded while the introduction of personnel policy, managerial skills, awarding talented staff, and reducing the proportion of officials on temporary contracts or secondments have contributed to an upgrading of the merit-based principles (Nugent 2001; Egeberg 2006b). By buttressing Weberian principles in the organization, the Commission's bureaucracy had to become a more unitary actor and in the process come to resemble national administrations more closely (Hooghe 2001: 200).

The internal reform had important implications for the job of senior officials. Increasingly they are expected to take up a more '*managerial*' role and a reconfigured policy role; to fulfil new skill requirements and to live up to enhanced expectations for political responsiveness. Changes in the Commission's financial management intended to give senior official more autonomy and flexibility in their work but also more responsibility. Performance demands make it, generally speaking, clearer what top-managers are accountable for and performance indicators may provide criteria against which they can be judged. The emphasis on the individual responsibility of directors general, combined with new promotion and grading procedures and the emphasis on results marked the shift to a new management culture.

Strengthening the core

The reforms in the Commission brought also a strengthening of the center over the organization and the policy process. Under Barroso's leadership the Commission has turned into a less fragmented and intergovernmental body. The increased powers of the Commission President and his cabinet have constrained the autonomy of the individual Commissioners and the DG's. The Secretariat-General (SG), which supports the work of the college has been strengthened as a part of the reform process. This has contributed to the creation of a powerful centre under the President, providing firm leadership and a political steer to the work of the Commission (Kassim & Menon 2004: 100). Stronger management from the center increased the 'cohesiveness' of the organization. Moreover, with the establishment of the *Strategic Planning and Programming* (SPP) cycle – concentrating on the setting of political priorities and the appropriate allocation of resources – the Commission not only intended to provide a framework to encourage performance oriented management, but also to provide for a larger control over the policy process from the center.

Streamlining the political-bureaucratic divide

Like several national ministers in Europe, each commissioner has his or her own political secretariat or private office. This cabinet of personally appointed officials, is organizationally separate from the administrative services. They constitute the link between the bureaucratic Commission and the political Commission. Common complaints in the Commission's permanent services, under both Delors and Santer, were that the cabinets mismanage this sensitive gate keeping functions and interfered far too aggressively and directly in the work of the departments (CIE 1999; 7.12.2 & 7.12.3). The cabinets were too closely associated with the interest and priorities of member governments, thus violating the commitment of the Commission to the 'common European good' (Peterson 2004).

The internal reforms had to diminish the political interference by cabinets in the work of the service; and intended to limit the numbers of cabinet staff and to make the presence in each cabinet of officials from at least three nationalities a requirement to constrain the possibilities for favouritism to which the cabinet structures gave rise. This marked a significant break from the past, when each cabinet was required to include only one non-national. Streamlining the organization of the Commission's political-administrative interface, by reducing the size and constraining the composition of the cabinets, intended to (re)assert control over the communications at the apex of the Commission.

Finally, the introduction of a new *Code of Conduct* provided for clear working relationships between the political and administrative levels at the apex and specified the distinctions between the respective responsibilities. The general principle is that Commissioners have to assume full political responsibility. Directors general are answerable to their Commissioner for the sound implementation of the policy guidelines laid down by the Commission.

A shifting administrative culture

The Commission's administrative culture moved from a rather closed one, with its roots in the Continental Franco-German tradition in the direction of a more open system associated with the Anglo-Saxon and Scandinavian models

(Balint et al. 2007). With previous enlargements, these 'new' national traditions have left their mark in the 'culture' of the Commission administration. Reforms in which the emphasis is on performance in the provision of services, responsiveness to the citizens, effectiveness and accountability are clearly visible. After the British and the Scandinavian countries entered the Commission they have brought with them a greater commitment to openness and equal opportunities for men and women (Stevens and Stevens 2006). The 10+2 enlargement diluted the existing patterns of different national cultures even further and provided a climate for the development of a more 'European' administrative culture.

6 Conclusion

Faced, at the end of the 1990s, with a decline in the Commission's power, legitimacy and credibility political leaders of the institutions of the EU and the member States have been engaged to put their 'House' in order (Cram 2002: 310). New structures and rules with a range of ex ante constraints and ex post and incentives have been created to enable an increased political control and influence in the Commission over its political executive and its administration. Clarifying structures and rules to retain the political *responsibility* for what happens within the Commission were an answer to its *control problem*. Enhancing the *responsiveness* of the Commission to the European Parliament and the European general public was necessary to fix its *legitimacy problem*. Meanwhile the Commission also engaged in attempts to ensure adequate resources and management capacity within the institution itself to oversee and support implementation capacities as an answer to its *management problems*. The evolution of the Commission is best characterized as a response and adaptation of an institution to internal impulses and an increasingly demanding and changing political environment.

The European Parliament has become a far more vociferous and demanding interlocutor and has contributed to the design of a more politically accountable Commission. This has placed greater pressure on Commissioners to control their administrative directorates. What is more, the work of the Commission has become more and more focussed on being 'responsive' to the interests of European citizens and to develop a more pronounced relationship with external actors such as the European public and the European parliament. Also, the College of commissioners, in its composition and in its organizational and recruitment procedures, has become more 'political' and less technocratic, whereas the appointments at the top of the commission bureaucracy has been increasingly 'depoliticized' by filling permanent positions by persons recruited on a merit basis. The internal reforms brought a more efficient and well managed bureaucracy that was more responsible and more responsive to the College of commissioners. In the end this has resulted in a clearer demarcation of the political and the administrative parts. These changes point to a European

Commission originally created as a technocratic body, but now gradually evolving into a regular core executive (Egeberg 2006b).

The Commission enhanced its autonomy vis-à-vis national governments over the years and issues of accountability, legitimacy and political control have become more central to the work of the Commission. This is not unexpected. The EU political order has evolved almost to the point that there is virtually no area of political or social life that is potentially not within its remit. The proliferation of activities of the EU into a political union – whose policies go far beyond the original aims of eliminating barriers to cross border economic activities – has strengthened the call for democratically legitimated decision-making and democratic accountability of European policy makers. Both political and administrative reforms are likely to yield a stronger, more dynamic, more modern, high performance policy focussed Commission that is now in a stronger position to do the job given to it by its EU founders (Peterson 2008). The irony is that the performance of the successfully reformed Commission appears to determine its own fate and future less and less. Elementary decisions, about the European integration process and the Commission's role in it, appear progressively more to be taken in national capitals, and over this the Commission has very little say.

References

Balint, T. & M.W Bauer & C. Knill, 2007. Bureaucratic Change in the European Administrative Space – The Case of the European Commission, in: M. Egeberg (ed.), *Institutional Dynamics and the Transformation of Executive Politics,* Mannheim: Connex Report Series Nr. 03, pp. 43-82.

Cini, M. 2000. *Organizational Culture and Reform: the case of the European commission under Jacques Santer,* European University Institute Working Papers, RSC 2000/25.

Christiansen, T. 1997. Tensions of European Governance: politicized bureaucracy and multiple accountability in the European Commission, *Journal of European Public Policy,* 4 (1): 73-90.

Christiansen, T. 2001. Intra-institutional politics and inter-institutional relations in the EU: towards coherent governance? *Journal of European Public Policy,* 8: 747-769.

Committee of Independent Experts, *First Report on Allegations regarding Fraud, Mismanagement and Nepotism in the European Commission* (15 March 1999), Brussels.

Cram, L. 2002. Introduction to Special Issue on the Institutional Balance and the Future of EU Governance: the Future of the Union and the Trap of the 'Nirvana Fallacy', *Governance,* 15 (3): 309-324.

Dimitrakapoulos, D.G. & H. Kassim, 2005. Inside the European Commission: Prefernce Formation and the Convention of the Future of Europe, *Comparative European Politics* (3): 180-203.

Egeberg, M. 1996. Organization and nationality in the European Commission services, *Public Administration,* 74: 721-35.

Egeberg, M. 2006a.The College of Commissioners: Executive Politics as Usual? in; M. Egeberg. *Multilevel Union Administration. The transformation of Executive Politics in Europe,* London: Palgrave MacMillan, pp. 51-65.

Egeberg, M. 2006b. Balancing Autonomy and Accountability: Enduring Tensions in the European Commission Development, in; M. Egeberg. *Multilevel Union Administration. The transformation of Executive Politics in Europe,* London: Palgrave MacMillan, pp. 31-50.

Euractiv.com, *Will Wallström's 'plan D' revive the European dream?* http://www.euractiv.com/en/governance/wallstrom-plan-revive-european-dream/article-144593, Published: Wednesday 21 September 2005 | Updated: Thursday 22 June 2006

Fouilleux; E., J.de Maillard & A. Smith (2005) Technical or political? The working groups of the EU Council of Ministers, Journal of European Public Policy, Vol 12 (4): 609-623.

Georgakis, D. & M. de Lasalle 2007. *Who are the Directors-General? European Construction and Administrative Careers in the Commission,* paper EU-Consent Network of Excellence, EU-Consent workshop, 'The Commission and the European Civil Service'.

Hix, S. 2004. The New Political Balance-of-Power in the European Union, *E!Sharp,* September issue.

Hix, S. 2006. Why the EU needs (left-Right) Politics? Policy Reform and Accountability are Impossible without it. *Politics: the Right or the Wrong Sort of Medicine for the EU?* Notre Europe, Policy paper no. 19, March 2006, http://www.notre-europe.asso.fr.

Hooghe, L & G. Marks, 2005. The Neofunctionalists Were (almost) Right: Politicization and European Integration, Constitutionalism WEB-papers, CONWEB 5/2005, http://www.qub.ac.uk/schools/SchoolofPoliticsInternationalStudiesandPhilosophy/FileStore/ConWEBFiles/Filetoupload,16451,en.pdf.

Hooghe, L. 2001. *The European Commission and the Integration of Europe*, Cambridge, Cambridge University Press.

Harlow, C. 2002. *Accountability in the European Union*. Oxford: Oxford University Press.

Judge, D & D. Earnshaw. 2002. The European Parliament and the Commission Crisis; A New Assertiveness? *Governance*, 15 (3): 345-374.

Kassim, H. 2004. A historic accomplishment? The Prodi Commission and administrative reform, in: *D.G. Dimitrakopoulos (ed), The Changing European Commission*, Manchester University Press, 33-62.

Kassim, H. 2006. The Secretariat General of the European Commission, in: D. Spence (ed.), *The European Commission*, London: John Harper Publishing.

Kassim, H. & A. Menon, 2004. EU Member States and the Prodi Commission, in: *D.G. Dimitrakopoulos (ed), The Changing European Commission*, Manchester University Press, 89-104.

Majone, G. 2002. The European Commission: the Limits of Centralization and the Perils of Parliamentarization, *Governance*, 15 (3): 374-392.

MacMullen, A. 2000. European Commissioners, in: N. Nugent (ed). *At the Heart of the Union, Studies of the European Commission*, London: Palgrave.

Nugent, N. 2001. *The European Commission*, Basingstoke: Palgrave.

Page, E. 1997. *People who Run Europe*, Oxford: Clarendon Press.

Peterson, J. 2004. The Prodi Commission: Fresh start or Free Fall, in: *D.G. Dimitrakopoulos (ed), The Changing European Commission*, Manchester University Press, 15-32.

Peterson, J. 2006. Where does the Commission stand today? in: D. Spence (ed.), *The European Commission*. London: John Harper Publishing, pp. 502-519.

Peterson, J. 2008. Enlargement, Reform and the Commission: Weathering a Perfect Storm? *Journal of European Public Policy*, 15 (5): 761-780.

Pollit, C. & Bouckaert, G. 2004 (2 ed). *Public Management Reform. A comparative analysis*. Oxford: Oxford University Press.

Spence, D. 2006. The president, the college and the cabinets. In: D. Spence (ed.), *The European Commission*. London: John Harper Publishing, pp. 25-74.

Stevens H. & A. Stevens. 2006. The Internal Reform of the Commission, In: D. Spence (ed.), The European Commission. London: John Harper Publishing, pp. 454-480.

Tsakatika, M. 2005. Claims to Legitimacy: the European Commission between continuity and Change, *Journal of Common Market Studies*, 43, (1): 193-220.

Trondal, J. 2004. Political dynamics of the parallel administration of the European Commission. In: A. Smith (ed) *Politics and the European Commission: Actors, interdependence, legitimacy*. London: Routledge. pp. 67-82.

Van Gerven, W. 2007. Legal, ethical, political and financial responsibility of EU Commissioners, Paper Presented for Committee on Budgetary Control, European Parliament, October 4, 2007.

Westlake, M. 2006. The European Commission and the European Parliament, in: D. Spence (ed.), *The European Commission*. London: John Harper Publishing, pp. 263-278.
Wonka, A. 2007. Technocratic and independent? The appointment of European Commissioners and its policy implications, *Journal of European Public Policy*, 14:2, 169-189.

CHAPTER 10

The European Commission in the Early 21st Century

Some Reflections on 'Politicians, Bureaucrats and the Reinvention of the European Commission' by Anchrit Wille

Thomas Christiansen

In the first decade of the 21st Century the European Commission has undergone a quiet revolution, a development that Anchrit Wille expertly charts in her contribution to this volume. It is a trajectory that has the potential to further exacerbate the already existing tensions inside the institution: at the political level, the 1999 'crisis' of the Santer Commission has reinforced the secular trend towards a greater 'parliamentarization' of the Commission, and at the administrative level the 'Kinnock reforms' that followed on from these same events were designed to insulate officials from the political influences that traditionally bear on the work of the Commission. In other words, the college of Commissioners has (had to) become more responsive to the political priorities of the day, while the services of the Commission are expected to be less politically responsive. Considering the inherent tension between such trends, it is remarkable that, as Wille attests, the Commission has become "more dynamic and [...] policy-focused, [being in 2008] in a stronger position to do the job".

At the same time however, we have also witnessed a European Commission that has been increasingly powerless in the process of treaty reform that has overshadowed much of the past decade. As Wille says, "the Commission [today] has very little say [...] [over] elementary decisions about the European integration process and [its] role in it." Long gone are the days of Delors, when the Commission was setting the agenda on treaty reform and the general direction of the Union. Instead, the Baroso Commission's declared focus on a 'Europe of results', coming after the futile attempt of the Prodi Commission to upgrade its status as a 'European government', appears as an admittance that the Commission has been a loser in the constitutional game. If, as it seems now, the drive towards explicit constitutionalization of the Union is over for the foreseeable future, then this is probably greeted with relief in certain quarters of the Commission.

The European Commission, even one that is becoming more politicised, remains uncomfortable with 'high politics' and continues to draw its power from the expertise it commands in the 'everyday politics' of the policy-process. And it is in this arena that the Commission's services have strengthened now that the opportunity costs of administrative reforms have been digested and resources are being better matched with objectives. Nevertheless, the challenges here also remain, considering that the administrative implications of EU enlargement have probably not yet trickled down, implying more work for the Commission both internally (in adapting to the more diverse background of its staff) and externally (in maintaining the compliance with EU legislation in the enlarged Union).

Indeed, even if both enlargement and treaty reform appear to be processes that have run their course, it would be safer to assume that these will continue to define the future of the European institutions of the next decade. Enlargement is a process that is still ongoing, given that the EU is actively negotiating with Croatia and Turkey, and has also opened the door to potential membership to the countries of the Western Balkans. As regards treaty reform, the Lisbon

Treaty may be in limbo at the end of 2008, but it is fair to assume that it will not just go away, even if there is no quick solution to the 'Irish problem'. If and when the Treaty is ratified, it will imply massive changes to the EU legislative process, and to the Commission's relations with Council (Secretariat) and European Parliament. And even if it ultimately does not come into force, both Lisbon Treaty and Constitutional Treaty will remain a reservoir of ideas that may fuel expectations and influence political choices down the road.

One concrete example of this dynamic – that of the introduction of 'delegated acts' in the new treaty – is worth mentioning here, given how much it is likely to impact on the Commission's work in the future. The Constitutional Treaty did establish this new legal instruments, which was foreseen as a tool for the European Commission to implement centrally EU legislation. It provided an alternative mechanism to the use of implementing acts, which the Commission can only adopt after having gone through 'comitology' – the system of implementing committees that allow Member States' representatives to scrutinise the way in which the Commission is using such delegated powers.

Comitology is a mechanism that has worked with considerable efficiency over the past 40 years, allowing the Commission to adopt thousands of implementing acts every year. It is, however, a system that the EP has been highly critical of, considering that the control is ultimately reserved to the Member States, even in those areas of co-decided legislation where *both* Parliament and Council have joint 'ownership' of the delegation of powers to the Commission. The creation of delegated acts in the Constitutional Treaty aims to rectify this incongruence by doing away with comitology committees and instead giving both legislative institutions direct and immediate powers to object to the adoption of any such delegated act by the Commission. Thus, if the Commission were empowered to use delegated acts in order to implement EU legislation, the equality of Parliament and Council as legislators would be reproduced in the implementation stage by both of them having equal powers to veto (and thereby indirectly control) the European Commission.

The innovation of the 'delegated acts' was in no small part due to the European Convention, where a working group chaired by Guiliano Amato drafted the relevant article, which was then introduced in the Draft Treaty and subsequently adopted, with minor changes, in the course of the Intergovernmental Conference. It was thus seen as an achievement by parliamentarians (who, after all, were the most numerous constituent group in the European Convention) to gain a foothold in an area that has hitherto been the preserve of the executive. At the same time, it appeared as a way of balancing the efficiency gains of delegated powers and the centralized implementation by the Commission with the need to hold the Commission accountable for policy-implementation and thereby enhancing the legitimacy of a system that is often regarded as obscure and overly technocratic.

If the creation of the new legal instrument of delegated acts was an acceptable compromise between Member States and European Parliament, then the maintenance of the status quo which resulted from the rejection of the Constitutional Treaty at the hands of the Dutch and the French voters was clearly not acceptable to the EP, which is why it started a campaign for legislative reform of the comitology system soon after the failure of ratification became evident in the second half of 2005. This drive for legislative reform resulted in a new 'Comitology Decision' in June 2006 which added a new procedure – the 'Regulatory Procedure with Scrutiny' also known by its French acronym PRAC – to the portfolio of comitology procedures. This new procedure – which, incidentally, was fundamentally different from the reform the Commission itself had proposed in 2002 – creates new opportunities for genuine parliamentary scrutiny and indeed veto of Commission implementing acts. Over time, it may bring about a transformation in the nature of the Commission's delegated powers, given that it provides for the regular referral of draft implementing measures to both Council and Parliament, irrespective of the opinion of the comitology committee. Thus a previously extremely rare event – legislative institutions engaging with the details of implementation – is set to become a much more regular occurrence, which in turn might open the doors for a greater politicization of EU policy-implementation.

To be sure, the use of such opportunities is bound to be selective, and the new procedure introducing the possibility of an EP veto over implementing acts is only being introduced gradually into both old parts of the *acquis* and new legislative acts, but this new procedure has already been applied quite widely and in some key areas of the EU's legislative activity (e.g. Services Directive, REACH Directive, Schengen legislation, financial services regulation). What remains unclear is the degree to which the EP will actually use its new powers, and delay or even block the implementation of EU legislation, and what mechanisms the Commission will develop in order to consult in advance with the European Parliament in order to draft executive acts that then do *not* meet with objections. The new comitology procedure certainly has the potential to make a significant impact on the way in which the Commission uses delegated powers, will lead to greater coordination between Commission, Council and EP in the implementation stage and is therefore likely to also politicise the world of comitology – a part of the EU's administrative system that so far has been remained largely de-politicised.

Comitology may or may not be an interesting battleground of inter-institutional relations in the Union, but this example demonstrates the degree to which the European Commission is subject to pressures from the other institutions, irrespective of whether the formal reform of the treaty goes ahead or not. As this case shows, even the failed attempt to devise a 'European Constitution' has ultimately had serious consequences for the work of the European Commission. This supports Wille's statement that it is ironic that the "successfully reformed Commission appears to determine it's own fate less and less". One might add that it is also ironic that the services of the Commission, recently reformed and expected to work in a much more managerial manner, are now expected to anticipate the political preferences of the EP when implementing policies. It remains to be seen whether this kind of 'politicisation by the back door' will ultimately do more harm than good to the legitimacy of the Commission as an independent institution.

If the role of the Commission as an agenda-setter is challenged in this way in the realm of 'low politics' to which comitology belongs, then the same is true when it comes to the broader agenda-setting in the European Union. Increasingly, the reflex of looking to the European Union for solutions to political, economic and social problems is *not* followed by a reflex of looking to the European Commission as the provider of such solutions. The EU's response during the 2008 financial crisis, when the larger Member States took the initiative and the French Presidency proposed a new regime for economic governance to be established outside the Commission, is just one case in point.

Reinvention of the European Commission may have come a long way over the past decade, as many aspects of the nature of administration have improved in the services of the European Commission and the President and the college of Commissioners have increased their political weight, but in relation to the other institutions, the Commission still falls short of its earlier aspirations. Perhaps it is crucially the *relative* nature of development that the Commission has undergone: while the Commission may have managed to improve its internal procedures and efficiency, both Council of Ministers and European Parliament have fared better (i.e. gained more powers and/or made better use of their prerogatives) during a turbulent decade, and in the end the Commission is seen to have lost ground in terms of the inter-institutional triangle. Time will tell whether a 'Europe of results' will also result in a return of the European Commission to the leading role it used to play in the integration process.

CHAPTER II

Some Remarks Concerning Commissioners

Collective Responsibility in Context, Temporary Committees of Inquiry, Political Independence and Neutrality

Walter van Gerven

I have been asked to make a contribution from a viewpoint of personal experience, as 'ervaringsdeskundige'. My experience with the Commission has been brief but decisive. It occurred during the period from February 2 to March 15 1999 when I was appointed by the European Parliament to sit with four others on a "Committee of Independent Experts" (hereinafter "the Committee"). The Committee was convened to investigate allegations raised in the European Parliament "regarding fraud, mismanagement and nepotism in the European Commission" (then under the presidency of Mr. Santer). The terms of reference restricted the Committee's mandate to six files (Tourism, Med programmes, ECHO, Leonardo da Vinci, the Security office and Nuclear Safety) and some allegations of nepotism, and concerned only the members of the Commission, not its civil servants. The report (hereinafter called "first report") was submitted to the European Parliament on 15 March 1999 at 5:00 p.m.,[1] and was followed the same day, around midnight, by the Commission's voluntary resignation. It is in that specific context that I would like to raise three points.

1. The first point is a general one and concerns the sentence in the last paragraph of the Committee's first report (under 9.4.25), which has drawn considerable attention from the media. The sentence reads: "It is becoming difficult to find anyone who has even the slightest sense of responsibility." Obviously, as such, the sentence could not to be documented by hard evidence and was rather to be understood as a "cri de coeur". To see that, it suffices to read the two preceding sentences stating: "Each individual must feel accountable for the measures he or she manages. The studies carried out by the Committee have too often revealed a growing reluctance among the members of the hierarchy to acknowledge their responsibility." In fact, it echoes statements made by some Commissioners when interviewed by the committee, saying: "Yes, I understand that this or that was going wrong but that was not *my* department" – a reply that the committee was not prepared to condone. According to the Committee, Commissioners bear a *collective responsibility* for behaviour of a colleague as of the moment that it can be proven, on the basis of a precise chronology of the facts, that first the Secretary General of the Commission, and then the President of the Commission, knew or could have known what went wrong in the department of one or another Commissioner, and that, subsequently, also the other Members were informed of the problem at Commission meetings, or through

[1] After having submitted its report to the European Parliament on 15 March 1999, the committee was commissioned by the Parliament to prepare a *second report*, this time not on precise allegations of "fraud, mismanagement and nepotism in the Commission" but "On the Reform of the Commission". That report which contained 90 concrete recommendations was submitted to the European Parliament on 10 September 1999 (hereinafter "the second report") and has been at the basis of a series of reforms undertaken by the new Commission under the Presidency of Mr. Prodi. See further Paul Craig, *EU Administrative Law*, Oxford University Press, 2006, 16-23.

their cabinets. That, of course, is based on the assumption that the Commission functions as a real team, as it should.[2]

To put things in perspective, some factual elements should be recalled. One is that the task of the Committee has been considerably facilitated by the fact that the main defaults retained by the Committee at the charge of Mrs. Cresson – the Commissioner (and her department) who appeared to be the most involved in cases of nepotism and mismanagement (as was later on confirmed by the ECJ[3]) were brought forward by a *whistleblower*, Mr. Van Buitenen. That is why the Committee in second report[4] underlined the usefulness of *whistleblowing* and the necessity for the hierarchy, as a signal of open government, to take *whistleblowers* seriously and to enact a proper framework for them.[5] Another fact is that, on the side of Commissioners, the Committee did not find corruption, but found (only) one case of nepotism and some cases of mismanagement. Corruption was however found in some of the Commission services (the Tourism and the ECHO files).[6] These findings are in stark contrast to the allegations about "sleaze" in the media, especially the tabloids. Furthermore, it is interesting to note that of the six files investigated by the Committee, only one originated under the presidency of Mr. Santer, the others originating under the presidency of Mr. Delors. In that context, the Committee found an obvious link – and delicate balance to be struck – between the need for the Commission to be creative in accepting new tasks and missions, on the one hand, and the requirement, on the other, to remain within budgetary limits certainly in periods of zero growth imposed by the Council of Ministers. In that respect, the behaviour of Member States is often ambiguous: on the one hand, they ask for creativity but, on the other hand, they insist on budgetary discipline. A combination of both requirements frequently results in an appeal to the private sector ('outsourcing') through procurement contracts, which do not always allow the administration to properly supervise the operation of private actors who, moreover, have often a lesser sensitivity for the general interest. In such circumstances, the combination of creativity and zero growth may sometimes works out as an incentive to initiate fraudulent practices.[7]

---

2 Collective responsibility and vicarious responsibility of the Commissioners (that is political responsibility towards the Parliament for behavior of their civil servants) are issues that have been discussed with many other accountability issues in the second report in chapter 7, particularly at sections 7.8, 7.10 and 7.14.

3 Case C-432/04, *Commission v. Cresson*, [2006] ECR I-6387.

4 Second report, supra n. 1, at paras. 7.6.8-7.6.10.

5 The new Commission under Mr. Prodi acted accordingly through its Commissioner Neil Kinnock: see *Raising Concerns about serious wrongdoings*, Consultative document of November 29, 2000, SEC (2000) 2078.who.

6 First report, Chapters 2 and 4.

7 For an analysis of service delivery and accountability, see Paul Craig, supra n. 1, at 12-16.

2. A second point concerns the formation of the Committee. In light of Article 193 EC, it is strange that the European Parliament has had recourse to the formation of an 'ad hoc' Committee of Independent Experts. Indeed, article 193 EC provides that:

> "[i]n the course of its duties the European Parliament may, at the request of a quarter of its Members, set up a *temporary Committee of Inquiry* to investigate, without prejudice to the powers conferred by this Treaty on other institutions or bodies, alleged contraventions or mal-administration in the implementation of Community law, except where the alleged facts are being examined before a court and while the case is till pending to legal proceedings ... The detailed provisions governing the exercise of the right of inquiry shall be determined by common accord of the European Parliament, the Council and the Commission." (emphasis added).[8]

These provisions had been applied for the first time in 1996 to look into transit fraud in the EU,[9] and a second time – after detailed provisions for holding inquiries had been laid down in an inter-institutional agreement between the European Parliament, the Council, and the Commission of 19 April 1995[10] – to examine the spread of BSE ("mad cow disease").[11] As a result of that second inquiry, the Commission's Directorate General underwent significant changes and, even more basically, a fundamental change of the legal basis for EC legislation in the field of veterinary medicine was agreed at the 1996/97 IGC.[12] On the negative side, some difficulties arose mainly because of the lack of coordination or even interaction between the European inquiry and a parallel UK inquiry,[13]

8 It is for the European Parliament to determine the composition and the rules of procedure of these committees: K. Lenaerts and P. Van Nuffel, *Constitutional Law of the European Union*, second ed., Thomson, 2005, at 398.

9 European Parliament, Report of the Committee of Inquiry into Community Transit System, A4-0053/97 (19 Feb. 1997); [1996] O.J. C7/1; identical version in C17/47.

10 Decision 95/167/EC, Euratom, ECSC of the European Parliament, the Council, and the Commission of April 19, 1995 on the detailed provisions governing the exercise of the European Parliament's right of inquiry, [1995] O.J. L113/2, appended to the EP Rules of Procedure as Annex VIII. See for a short overview, with references, K. Lenaerts and P. Van Nuffel , supra n. 8, at 397-398.

11 [1996] O.J. C239/1. On this inquiry, see Carol Harlow, *Accountability in the European Union*, Oxford University Press, 2002, p. 99-100. The inquiry has led to important reactions from the Commission, under pressure of the EP which had warned the Commission that, if the Committee's recommendations were not carried out within a reasonable deadline and in any event by November 1997, a motion of censure would be tabled. See also A. Maurer, 'The European Parliament between Policy making and Control' in: *Debating the democracy of the European Union* (B. Kohler-Koch and B. Rittberger, eds.), Rowman et al., Lanham, 2007, at 96.

12 C. Harlow, supra n. 11, at 100.

13 Ibid.

showing that, as in many other areas, there is an urgent need for adequate cooperation between Union and national levels.[14]

Committees of inquiry are a popular device in the *UK and Ireland* where tribunals of inquiry are used to scrutinize complex cases of ministerial misconduct, and are seen as an essential instrument to interrogate cabinet ministers, including the Prime Minister, and civil servants.[15] It is a flexible (but expensive) instrument, as it is for the chairman, usually a senior judge, to decide how to conduct the inquiry, who to call as witnesses and how long the inquiry will take. Strangely enough – probably because of political deadlock at the time between the two major political parties[16] – and also regrettably, the procedure of *Article 193 EC* was not followed by the European Parliament in 1999. If used, it might have prevented the Commission from resigning voluntarily immediately after the report came out, and, instead, might have induced the Commission to appear before Parliament to answer questions, justify its behaviour and, eventually, contradict the Committee's findings, or some of them. That would have constituted a precedent for the future in that it supplied the European Parliament with an important tool to exercise its control function in an efficient manner, that is, by hearing the Commission out (as well as the Committee) in a public session. Moreover, the use of Article 193 EC instead of an 'ad hoc' procedure would have made it unnecessary for the Committee to examine its own legally doubtful status and jurisdiction.[17]

Not only the status and jurisdiction of the Committee were uncertain; also the rules that the Committee was bound to apply in assessing the Commissioners' behaviour were unknown to the Committee when it started its investigations. A major question before it at its first meeting was, for example, whether the Commissioners' conduct had to be assessed only on the basis of what in French administrative law are called *irrégularités administratives*, or whether the Committee should also take into account ethical rules, or codes of conduct. After some discussion the Committee took the view that the latter was to be

---

14 More recently, the procedure has been used again to investigate "the crisis of the Equitable Life Assurance Society" in which case a resolution was adopted on 19 June 2007.

15 A recent illustration is the tribunal set up to inquire into the suicide of Dr. Kelly, the British expert who had said to a journalist that the Blair administration was responsible for consciously misleading the public on the issue of weapons of mass destruction in Iraq. See W. Van Gerven, *The European Union. A Polity of States and Peoples*, Stanford University Press and Hart Publishing Oxford, 2005, at 74.

16 See S. Douglas-Scott, *Constitutional Law of the European Union*, Longman, 2002, at 71-72. It would seem that the two main European political parties -the EPP and the Socialist Party- did not agree on the course to follow, the EPP wanting only Mrs. Cresson to be sent away (she was a former socialist prime minister of France), whilst the Socialist Party wanted to have the whole Commission resign (including its President, Mr. Santer, who was a former Christian Democrat Prime Minister of Luxembourg). To avoid such a deadlock at the moment of a political crisis, I have suggested elsewhere that, for the future, Parliament should set up a standing Committee of Inquiry at the beginning of each legislative period.

17 On this, see points 1.2.1 to 1.2.6 of the Committee's first report.

the case.[18] To flesh out the concept of proper ethical behaviour, the Committee sought inspiration in the Standards in Public life as applied in the UK by the Committee on Standards in Public Life. On the basis of that concept, the Committee defined a common core of 'minimum standards' around the principles of independence, integrity and discretion, and accountability and openness to the public. In its recommendations, the Committee suggested that a similar committee be installed at the European level by way of an inter-institutional agreement.[19] So far, the suggestion has not been followed but a modified Code of Conduct for Commissioners has been adopted by the Commission under Mr. Barroso on 24 November 2004.[20]

3. My third point concerns the *position of Commissioners*. Commissioners have a very ambiguous status: they are not civil servants but holders of public office – an undefined category; they are not politicians, at least not elected politicians, but most of them have been politicians in their own country in the past (and some may go back to national politics) – with the result that, while in office, they are still perceived as politicians by the people (and often behave themselves as politicians). The ambiguity of the position was raised by Mrs. Cresson before the Court of Justice who tried to use the difference in position to her advantage. She pointed out that "an official of the European Communities benefits from considerably more extensive safeguards than those provided for Members of the Commission, both at the stage of the administrative procedure and in proceedings before the Court."[21] The latter is particularly true in that "an official may challenge a decision of the Appointing Authority before the Court of First Instance ... and then bring an appeal before the Court of Justice" (both quotations in para. 86) whereas a Commissioner lacks "any opportunity to challenge the decision of the Court of Justice which, according to Mrs Cresson constitutes a breach of fundamental rights" (ibid.). The Court acknowledged the fact but did not accept the argument that this constituted a breach of her fundamental rights for which the Court referred to Article 2 (2) of Protocol no. 7 to the ECHR. That article provides in an exception to the requirement of two levels of jurisdiction, "where the person concerned was tried in the first instance by the highest court or tribunal" (para. 112).

Since Commissioners are not subjected to staff regulations, for better or for worse, one has to rely on the Treaty provisions to know their obligations. Thus, in Article 213 (1) and (2) EC, it is stated that the independence of Commissioners must be beyond doubt which means that, in the performance of their duties,

---

18 See points 1.4.1.to 1.5.4 of the Committee's first report.

19 See recommendation 81 in the Second Report.

20 The Commission under Mr. Barrroso has proposed the creation of an Advisory Group on Standards in Public Life, SEC (2000) 2077 but Parliament and Council have not given adequate attention to it according to the Commission.

21 See supra n. 3.

they shall neither seek or take instructions from any government, or from any other body. Moreover, they may not, during their term of office, engage in any other occupation, whether gainful or not. They shall give a solemn undertaking that they will behave with integrity and discretion as regards the acceptance, after they have ceased to hold office, of certain appointments or benefits. In the Cresson judgment, the ECJ has emphasized that the concept of 'obligations arising from their office' falls to be broadly construed. In the above quoted provision in Article 213 (2) EC, the terms "from any other body" and "not engage in any other occupation, whether gainful or not" may give rise to difficult questions, thus, for example whether and in how far Commissioners may take *instructions from political parties* and/or engage in *political activities* in their State of origin, or elsewhere. A delicate question in that respect is whether Commissioners, who are part of the Community's main policy-formulating and law-initiating body, are allowed to represent views advocated by a political party of which they are, or are perceived to be, a passive member, if not an active one.

In my opinion, the answer to that question is somewhere in the middle. On the one hand, it is clear that Commissioners who, without being a politician, carry out an essentially political function, may not be prevented from having a political view and expressing it in an independent and responsible – that is, not in a unnecessarily controversial or partisan – manner.[22] In other words, in *expressing* their views, Commissioners must check and weigh these against, and in light of, opposing reasonable views. It is therefore acceptable and desirable that, in the appointment of Commissioners, Member States seek to establish within the Commission a balanced representation of European political tendencies.[23] On the other hand, it should be equally clear that Commissioners may not seek *instructions*, not even occasionally, from a political party, whether national or European, on how to vote in the Commission on an issue that is politically controversial. Taking instructions from a political party would seem to me to be in conflict with the *neutrality*, which the function of Commissioner requires.

What about being an *active member* of a political party[24] and, more specifically, taking part in a national or European *election campaign* on behalf of a political party? In so far as these activities constitute an "occupation, gainful

---

22 According to the Commission, Members of the Commission are politicians carrying out a political function, who, while honouring the obligations imposed by their function, remain free to express their personal opinions quite independently and on their own responsibility: thus in answers to written questions particularly the answer of February 7, 2000 to questions E-2459/99, E-2600/99 and E-2628/99, [2000] OJ C255E/139 (taken from K. Lenaerts and P. Van Nuffel (R. Bray, ed.), *Constitutional Law of the European Union*, Thomson, 2nd. ed., 2005, at p. 435, fn. 247.

23 As has happened in the past: see P.J.G. Kapteyn and VerLoren van Themaat, ed. and rev. by L.W. Gormley, *Introduction to the Law of the European Communities*, Kluwer Law International, 3rd. ed., 1998, at 195, fn. 90.

24 In some Member States (the UK) civil servants in policy grades may not even be passive members of a political party: Kapteyn and VerLoren van Themaat (supra n. 21), at p. 200, fn. 112.

or not, outside the Commission" in the sense of Article 213 (2) EC – which in my opinion is to be understood as "taking up working time" – such activities are not allowed under the wording of the Treaty itself, and therefore cannot be deviated from. But even if they are not "occupational", for example because they are carried out during vacation periods, or sabbatical leave, I would still think that they should not be permitted for not being in conformity with the wording of the Treaty: to be an active member of a political party, or campaign for that party, implies in my view that the person concerned accepts the party line, and therefore is implicitly following instructions from the party.[25]

It is clear that the status of Commissioners as holders of public office can only be clarified when Commissioners are given the status of Ministers in a parliamentary democracy which means that they would normally be politicians elected by the people in parliamentary elections and then invited by a person who is charged to form a government and who will become prime minister, to take part in a government, in all probability a coalition government, that is supported by a majority in Parliament. However, that is not for to-morrow, if ever.[26]

[25] I know that my opinion is in conflict with the provisions of the 2004 Code of conduct for Commissioners (under point 1.1.1), as prepared by the Secretariat-General, Directorate B. However, I find my interpretation more in line with the text and the spirit of the Treaty, and with the terms "independence beyond doubt" in Article 213 (1) EC.

[26] See further W. Van Gerven, *The European Union. A Polity of States and Peoples*, supra n. 15, in chapter 7 on 'Which form of government for Europe?' at 350-352.

CHAPTER 12

The Council of Ministers: The Missing Link?

Deirdre Curtin

1 Introduction

The description of the Council of Ministers as the 'missing link' is not my description but that of the organizers of this conference. What is missing? With what is the link missing: with other levels of governance or with mechanisms of accountability? Is the link missing or is it just weak, weaker or weakest? If it is the weakest link does that imply as the popular BBC program of the same name that it can be eliminated from the equation entirely? Can I like Anne Robinson simply dismiss the Council of Ministers from the accountability stage, with no further ado? Or do we need to draw different conclusions and even conceive of more pro-active remedies to put back in a missing – or weak – link? A link after all fits in a chain with one assumes many more links that may even go in different directions. The title, provided that it is written with a question mark, throws up more than enough unclear and unresolved questions to function perfectly well as an additional topic to be separately addressed alongside the various different institutions that have been studied over the course of the past three years of this project.

Whatever about the correct adjective to be applied to the Council of Ministers it is in any event the specific and primary link between the EU political system and the national political systems.[1] Second, it may provide a link with the international legal system. Finally, if the Treaty of Lisbon comes into force later this year or next year it will link up very explicitly with what can be termed the supreme political actor in the EU political system: the European Council and its new-soon to be appointed – semi permanent President. Of course it already had other links in terms of legislative decision making above all both with the Commission and with the European Parliament. What is new is the closeness of the structural and institutional link with each of these three different levels: national, international and horizontal in the EU system itself. This raises different issues in terms of the manner in which the link with accountability in some fashion may be 'missing' or 'problematic'. I will now consider each of the three levels separately in an effort to undertake some evaluation and reach some tentative conclusions.

2 The Link with the National Political Systems: Political Representation

Let us dwell a moment on the *specific nature* of the Council of Ministers in the EU institutional configuration. Its most defining feature is that it is *intergovernmental* and that in this council the Member States are as such represented both individually and collectively, just as in virtually all other inter-

[1] See further on the 'chameleonic' nature of the Council of Ministers, D. Curtin, *Executive Power in the European Union: Law, Practices and the Living Constitution* (Oxford, Oxford University Press, 2009, forthcoming).

national organizations.[2] The Council of Ministers was originally conceived as *the* manner that the Member States could keep the constitutionally more autonomous Commission in its place to some extent. It was conceived as the central decision-maker that enabled the Member States individually and collectively to input into the EU political system as it developed over the years.[3] The Commission may have been conceived largely as a technocratic institution, the Council of Ministers was the *political* institution. The politics in question were those of the national political systems that were reflected in the fact that the representatives of the Member states were either elected directly or appointed by those that had been directly elected, the national parliaments.

I would like to explore this issue of *political representation* a moment. The political nature of the Council came from the fact that it was composed of members of the national executive power. But is its power 'politicized' in the sense we know from national political systems where elections take place on the basis of a system of political parties with left-right cleavages? And what do we mean by 'representation' in this context: are the ministers and civil servants really 'representing' the citizens when they take decisions at the EU level? Throughout Europe representation is commonly understood to work via the 'responsible party government' model, in which the electorate selects from two or more parties based on their policy promises and performance.[4] This mechanism provides a link between the preferences of citizens and the actions of governments. Parties in power remain accountable on a day-to-day basis to parliaments and at regular intervals to the electorate, who retain ultimate control. This model is – as is well known – highly problematic when applied in the context of the European Union both in the indirect channel (national elections) and the direct one (direct elections to the European Parliament).[5] At present we only find the conditions for electoral and party democracy at the national level and even these may be weakening, according to some analyses. This is precisely what Vivien Schmidt, refers to in her book, *Democracy in Europe:*[6] at the national level we find 'politics' but 'without policy'. In this case says Schmidt we are left with at the EU level: 'policy without politics'.

[2] See, T. Christensen, 'The Council of Ministers: The Politics of Institutionalised Intergovernmentalism', in: J. Richardson, *European Union: Power and Policy-Making* (Routledge, London, 2001), pp. 135-154, at p. 136.

[3] See, W. Wessels, 'The EC Council: The Community's Decision-making Centre', in: R.O. Keohane and S. Hoffmann (eds.), *The New European Community: Decision-making and Institutional Change (*Boulder CO, Westview, 1991) p. 133. See, in general terms, F. Hayes-Renshaw and H. Wallace, *The Council of Ministers* (second ed. Palgrave Macmillan, 2006).

[4] See further, M. March and P. Norris, 'Political Representation in the European Parliament', 32 *European Journal of Political Research* (1997), pp. 153-164.

[5] See further on the latter, M. Marsh and P. Norris, op cit and more recently and generally, C. van Eijk and H. Schmitt (eds), *The Multilevel Electoral System of the EU*, (CONNEX Report Series No. 4: Mannheim, 2008).

[6] See, V. Schmidt, *Democracy in Europe: The EU and National Polities* (Oxford, Oxford University Press, 2006), p. ix.

On this analysis therefore there is no unbroken chain linking the voting citizen through the national parliaments and government ministers to actual decision making in the Council of Ministers quite irrespective of the manner of voting in the Council via unanimity or qualified majority voting. The fact that the accentuated trend towards more and more qualified majority voting in Council decision making across very many policy areas only serves to highlight the broken chains both of delegation upwards and of accountability downwards. The Council of Ministers then is indeed the 'missing link' between the politics that stay at the national level and the policy that to a considerable and increasing degree takes place at the EU level. It is 'missing' and the chains are broken. On this reading then the Council of Ministers has an autonomous executive role at the level of the EU political level that has been 'depoliticized' to a considerable extent. Moreover that role played by members of the national executives is 'depoliticised' even in the manner that it exercises its crucial role in the overall legislative process. Let me now elaborate briefly on the role of the Council of Ministers as legislative decision taker in the EU legal and political systems.

3 The Council of Ministers as Legislature

As recently as 1997, just over a decade ago, the Council of Ministers was described as 'the most important law making body...essentially an intergovernmental negotiating forum representing Member States and acting behind closed doors.'[7] This was almost five years after the Treaty of Maastricht and sustained efforts to introduce more 'transparency' in EU decision-making, including by the Council of Ministers. One of the defining features of the Council of Ministers is that, by diplomatic negotiations, it distils the bottom line in terms of the collective of national interests. This process of reaching a decision traditionally took place behind closed doors with very little light being shed on the meetings as such. The processes of amendment of specific texts were often presented as necessary in order to enable the Council to reach decisions at all.[8] Considerable improvements have taken place in recent years as a result of a variety of 'transparency' provisions but nonetheless one often needs

7 See, P. Norris, 'Representation and the democratic deficit', 32 *European Journal of Political Research* (2007), pp. 273-282, at 273.

8 See for example, the Council refusal to John Carvel, endorsed by the General Affairs Council, 16 May 1994 (ten votes to two (the Netherlands and Denmark voting against)) informing him he could not have access to the JHA documents because: 'they refer directly to the deliberations of the Council and its preparatory instances. If it did allow access, the Council would fail to protect the confidentiality of its proceedings... [and] the position taken by the members of the Council during its deliberations' (cited in T. Bunyan, *Secrecy and Openness in the EU* (Kogan Page, 1999), pp. 14-15. Further, when Statewatch applied for a document in 2000 setting out far-reaching changes to the 1993 code of public access to EU documents in July (the 'Solana Decision') the Council refused and said its release 'could fuel public discussion on the subject'. See 'Essays for an Open Europe', http://www.statewatch.org/essays.pdf p5.

the mindset of a focused private investigator to unearth relevant information both about processes and about its various (sub-) actors. Even in 2009 it still remains 'shrouded' in secrecy in many salient respects. Moreover that secrecy has permeated the manner in which legislation is adopted at the EU level more generally especially as the European Parliament has acquired incrementally a more central role in co-decision.

Let me elaborate on this as it raises the link between the legislative role of the Council at the European level and the legislative role of the European Parliament at the European level. Once the Treaty of Lisbon enters into force *joint decision-making* by the two institutions will constitute the normal legislative procedure, with exceptionally ('specific legislative procedures') the Council fulfilling its decision-making role more autonomously.[9] The evolving partnership between the Council and the European Parliament is shaped however not only by formal treaty level reforms but also by the formal and informal arrangements made by both institutions to adapt to the altered inter-institutional circumstances.[10] The fundamental difference with pre-existing procedures involving some role for the European Parliament is that co-decision from the very beginning involved direct negotiations between Parliament and the Council. These negotiations are in fact largely governed by inter-institutional agreements rather than by formal legal or treaty provisions.[11] This can give rise to what has been called 'the growing cocoon of power'.[12]

Recent research has shown that the European Parliament has been a particularly successful constitutional agenda-setter in recent years and has successfully persuaded the Member States to grant it incrementally more equal legislative powers alongside the Council. In the words of Rittberger, 'once integration looms, normative pressure is generated to counter the threat which policy-makers in the EU associate with integration, namely that further integration undermines domestic democratic and institutions.'[13] The response has been to project the model of parliamentary democracy onto the European level.[14] The downside in the dominant legitimation strategy of involving the

9 For chapter and verse see R. Barents, *Het Verdrag van Lissabon: Achtergronden en commentaar* (Kluwer, Deventer, 2008).

10 See further, B. Driessen, *Interinstitutional Conventions in EU Law*, (Cameron & May, London, 2007), in particular Chapter 10.

11 See, B. Driessen, ibid. at p. 166.

12 See, S. Puntscher Riekmann, 'The Cocoon of Power: Democratic Implications of Interinstitutional Agreements', 13:1 *European Law Journal* (2007), pp. 4-19.

13 See, B. Rittberger, 'Constructing Parliamentary Democracy in the European Union: How Did It Happen?', in: B. Kohler-Koch and B. Ritberger (eds.), *Debating the Democratic Legitimacy of the European Union* (Rowman and Littlefield, Plymouth 2007), pp. 111-137, at 133.

14 Political scientists also cite other (more complex) explanations: for example the argument has been made that the European Parliament has been deliberately empowered as a co-legislator in the co-decision procedure because of the benefit that Member States putatively enjoy as a result because of the informational asymmetries between the Council and the European Parliament. The argument is made

European Parliament in a model of European parliamentary democracy has been the manner in which the Council of Ministers seems to have successfully influenced the European Parliament to shift a not insignificant part of its decision-taking on deliberations to behind closed doors 'negotiations'. This has to do with the manner in which the informal institution has evolved of so-called 'trialogue meetings' devised as an informal but structured means of bringing together a reduced number of participants by both sides (Council and European Parliament) in order to attempt to resolve contentious issues so that overall agreement (co-decision) could be brokered.[15] Initially it seems that the practice arose because of the failure of the (Maastricht) Treaty to say what should happen after the Council had given its view on the second reading amendments of the EP and before a 'conciliation committee' had been convened. It was considered a pragmatic and sensible way of preparing with a small group of people the major issues that needed to be addressed in full conciliation committee.

These unwritten rules, have in the words of insider Schackleton, 'served to make trialogues an extremely successful instrument: no one could now imagine the procedure without them. However they are not just an instrument to be applied where appropriate. They have affected the way in which each side views the other and fashioned common attitudes which have contributed to the resolution of differences.'[16] There is however more to it in terms of an evolving relationship: 'trialogues' once they enter the informal institutional panorama did not long remain confined to the post second reading, pre-conciliation phase, they increasingly came to be used at the first reading and early second reading stage.[17] When this is combined with the fact that the vast majority of all co-decision measures are now adopted at this stage then the implications may be more serious than was assumed in the relatively early days when their role was more circumscribed. It now appears from recent studies of how and when legislation is adopted in practice at the EU level that 80% of all agreements made under co-decision in the first 3 years of the current term of the European Parliament (2004-2007) were either agreed during the first reading (64%) or in an early second reading based on informal negotiations with resulting amendments directly integrated into the Council's common position.[18] A new joint declaration

that the introduction of co-decision benefits Member States *vis a vis* solutions under the consultation procedure in which a better informed Commission only needs to find the support of a qualified majority of Member States. See further, T.Koenig, 'Why do Member States empower the European Parliament?', 15:2 *JEPP* (2008) , pp. 167-188.

[15] See further on the origins of the practice, M. Schackleton, 'The Politics of Codecision', 38:2 *Journal of Common Market Studies* (2000), pp. 325-342.

[16] Ibid.

[17] This is acknowledged and indeed encouraged by the institution themselves. See the specific provisions of the Joint Declaration by the European Parliament, Council and Commission on practical arrangements for the co decision procedure, OJ C 145/5, points 7. 10 and 11.

[18] See further, S. Kurpas, C. Green and P. Maciej Kaczynski, 'The European Commission after Enlargement: Does More Add Up to Less?', CEPS Special Report, February 2008, www.ceps.be.

by the European Parliament, Council and Commission on 'practical arrangements for the codecision procedure' states that: 'the institutions shall cooperate in good faith with a view to reconciling their positions as far as possible so that, wherever possible, acts can be adopted at first reading'.[19] This attempt – since 1999 – to extend trialogues backwards to the first and second readings so as to make the early agreement system workable has been remarkably successful.

The first reading does not have a time limit and is typically less formal than the subsequent stages in the procedure. 'Trialogues' between representatives of the three institutions during first or early second reading help to identify common ground, and speed up the process but they also remove the subjects under discussion from the realm of open political debate within and between the institutions, with the potential involvement of the public. This potentially affects the function of parliament to adopt and deliberate on legislation in an open and public process. In this way the debate becomes de-politicised and enters the realm of closed inter-institutional 'negotiations'. There are increasingly concerns about a lack of transparency, democratic legitimacy and clarity on the procedural steps'.[20] The Council, on this reading is enabled to tie the European Parliament into its 'cocoon of power' – negotiations behind closed doors – even with a directly elected parliament. It has been facilitated by inter-institutional rule making in the interstices of the formal rules that seems to be particularly paradigmatic in the context of co-decision.[21]

There is much more evidence than previously that the Council and the European Parliament are working systematically together and attempting to closely network and take into account each other's preferences even in the very early stages.[22] The problem is that with the increase in the numbers of areas subject to co-decision the number of informal meetings going on at any one time on a de-central basis in the EP leads to 'an absolute maze' that will only proliferate further with the entry into force of the Treaty of Lisbon. They do not seem to be centrally co-coordinated, and even central figures in the EP might not know about all the meetings that are going on. In addition there is – according to insiders – little informal control of the work of the key negotiators internally within the Parliament.[23] At the same time there is some evidence that

---

19 OJ C 145/5 (30 june 2007).

20 CEPS Report, ibid. at p. 30. See too the concerns expressed in: European Parliament, *Conciliations and Co-decision: A Guide to how the Parliament Legislates* (Brussels, July 2007), http://www.europarl.europa.eu/code/information/guide_en.pdf.

21 See further. H. Farrell and A. Heretier, 'Formal and Informal Institutions under Co-Decision: Continuous Constitution-Building in Europe', 16:4 *Governance: An International Journal of Policy, Administration and Institutions* (2003), pp. 577-600.

22 See, H. Farrell and A. Heretier, op. cit.

23 See, A. Rasmussen and M. Shackleton, 'The scope for action of European Parliament negotiators in the legislative process: Lessons of the past and for the future', Paper prepared for the Ninth Biennial International Conference of the European Union Studies Association, Austin, Texas, March 31–April 2, 2005, http://aei.pitt.edu/2983.

the European Parliament is engaged in a strategy of sorts: to force the Council to come before Parliament and explain its views in committee, thereby forcing it to accept that it owes some accountability for its input into the legislative process to the European Parliament. The problem with this approach is that they are co-legislators and that in these circumstances it may well be difficult for the European Parliament to objectively hold the Council to account in some seriously substantive fashion in this highly specific institutional context.

A wiser strategy may be for the European Parliament, now that it has finally in the Lisbon Treaty acquired its pivotal status as legislative partner in the general legislative process to insist that it does not compromise on its *agora* function of ensuring that legislation is as far as possible taking place in an open public process and arena.

4 Concluding Remarks

In the twenty minutes allotted to my talk at the end of this very rich and interesting conference I have tried to raise the specific nature of the Council of Ministers and its links as an executive power to the legislative power at two levels: the national political level and the European political level. There is however much more to the nature of the Council of Ministers than has been possible to deal with in my brief presentation this afternoon. I have not touched upon the growing non-legislative role and status of the Council of Ministers. I mention them only now because I think it is inevitable that they be included in a further agenda for research.

There are two related aspects to the non-legislative power of the Council of Ministers: first, the manner in which the Secretariat General of the Council has acquired over the course of at least the past decade what can only be termed autonomous executive powers that in some ways parallel powers that the Commission would normally exercise.[24] This relates in particular to the new policy areas introduced in the Maastricht Treaty, CFSP and JHA. It entails not only exercise of powers of implementation but also administrative and management tasks and indeed the setting up of new structures within the Council Secretariat with specific powers and tasks. The endowment of the Council General Secretariat with *new* executive tasks has been particularly striking since the establishment of the European Security and Defense Policy and the appointment of Javier Solana as High Representative of the Common Foreign and Security Policy at the same time as being Secretary General of the Council Secretariat. It seems as if parts of the Council Secretariat have very incrementally and – on the whole – quietly developed features that are more similar to those found in executive offices than in classical secretariats. Its tasks include

[24] See further, D. Curtin, *Executive Power in the European Union: Law, Practices and the Living Constitution* (Oxford, Oxford University Press, 2009, forthcoming), Chapter 5.

agenda setting, policy formulation and implementation, especially in the fields of internal and external security.

In other words it can be argued that what has been happening in an incremental fashion over the course of the past ten years within the EU has been the development of two parallel administrations, each with their own (quasi-) independent 'satellites' (Community bodies/ Union bodies). The difference between the two 'strands' is that the Commission is embedded into an (imperfect) accountability system tailored to the types of decisions it takes and the powers it has and that the Council (and European Council) is not for the largely historic reason that it had to be conceptualised as an inter-governmental body whose Ministers had been elected and were accountable to national parliaments in the last resort. Moreover there has been traditionally surprisingly little focus on the Council's executive tasks as opposed to its legislative role. The fact that the latter has grown over the course of the past decade seems not only to have gone largely unnoticed but also not to have forced any serious challenge to the continuing validity of the claim that its indirect legitimacy via the national political process is adequate or tailored to the kinds of activities that take place under its institutional umbrella nor the types of decisions it takes far removed from any politicized public sphere.

The Council of Ministers has become institutionalised in recent years in a manner that transcends a purely inter-governmental – and political – understanding. In other words it has also acquired what can be called *an autonomous executive* role. This is true at various levels. It has been reinforced and consolidated in the new Treaty of Lisbon with the scope and role of the *political executive* greatly increased. Thus the *European Council* will acquire a semi-permanent President and be supported by the Council Secretariat; the Commission President sees his powers enhanced in certain respects and the EU acquires effectively an EU Foreign Minister, even if the latter has been renamed the High Representative for Foreign and Security Policy.

Taken as a whole the Lisbon Treaty does not aggravate the democratic deficit but improves it in a few distinct ways without by any means eliminating it. The rule of law is strengthened as a result of the more streamlined role given to the courts in Luxembourg in partnership with national courts. Finally, it makes more visible than was previously the case what the political system of the EU is, who the actors are, what their powers are and the nature of their decisions in language that can be compared to what happens in national political and constitutional systems. This does not mean that a super-state is being created, rather that we find at the European level the same phenomena that we find at the national level.

The national executive power has long operated outside of its own national political and constitutional level. It is active and engaged in decision making at the European level and at the international or global level. It has in a sense and as a matter of practice surmounted thinking in terms of hierarchical levels and may even be considered as engaged in a more fluid and composite governance process.[25] The core problem can be considered to be that outside of the confines of the territorial Nation States executives are only to a very limited extent held to *account* for their actions and inactions. While national parliaments have stayed put within their own neatly nationally fenced off compartments, the executive has developed into a strongly interwoven, complex administrative network, beyond the horizons of many, maybe all national parliaments.[26] There is no reason moreover why the national parliaments should restrict themselves to holding their own national representative to account. Why can the respective national parliaments not enjoy the privilege of a real and lively debate with the newly to be appointed President of the European Council? Why could there not be annual debate on the state of the Union in the respective national parliaments to hold the European institutions to account?

Parliaments need to stop feeling trapped within an enclosed national system and try and keep up with where power and rule making has migrated and play a role in holding it to account. None of these suggestions need constitutional amendments of treaty revisions but could in most cases be effectuated as a matter of bottom-up, pro-active practice by the national parliaments themselves. In my view this is the next stage of European integration that needs to be brought about by the actors in the national political systems themselves. Only then can we start linking in a less fragmentary fashion than currently the case national *politics* and European *policies*.

[25] See further, L. Besselink, *A Composite European Constitution*, (Europa Law Publishing, 2008).

[26] L. Besselink, ibid.

CHAPTER 13

Executive Accountability under the European Constitution and the Lisbon Treaty

Nihil Novi sub Sole?

Bruno de Witte

1 Introduction: The Absence of a Grand Institutional Reform

Executive accountability is particularly problematic in the European Union firstly because the traditional mechanisms of political accountability (control by the European Parliament on the Commission, and control by national parliaments on their own government acting within the Council) do not work very well, due to the nature of the EU system; and secondly, because of the greater remoteness of the European Union from the citizens. Moreover, the executive branch of the EU has increasingly become a 'many-headed monster'. The *European Commission* is still the core executive. It cumulates various executive roles: the initiation of legislation, the implementation of legislation with or without *comitology*, the monitoring of Member States compliance, and enforcement of competition rules against private firms. The *Council* also increasingly exercises executive functions (mainly under the second and third pillar). Next to these main institutions with executive powers, specialised executive functions are also exercised by the *European Central Bank*. Powers have been delegated both by the Commission and the Council to *agencies* and increasing recourse is had to forms of shared administration between the EU and the Member States: the *open method of coordination*, and the use of regulatory *networks*.

All these institutions and bodies exercise some form of executive authority and they require ever more sophisticated 'countervailing' mechanisms to ensure their accountability. In addition to judicial control by the European and national courts, and to political control by the European and national parliaments, we find other forums of accountability such as the Ombudsman. The rules on transparency and access to documents, although they are strictly speaking not accountability mechanisms, are seen as instrumental to the effective functioning of public accountability; access of documents is one area of accountability which has been shaped by the case law of the ECJ.

In this chapter, I build on the existing knowledge about all these elements of Europe's changing 'executive order'[1] and address the more narrow question of whether the 'accountability *acquis*' is likely to be modified, and if so on which points, by the possible entry into force of the Treaty of Lisbon in 2010.

At some moments during the decade-long Treaty reform process, which is now possible drawing to a close, it seemed possibly or even likely that there would be a major upheaval of the existing regime of executive power and accountability in the EU. The beginning of the process was inauspicious, though. At the Nice European Council of December 2000, the Heads of State and Government stated, in an annexed *Declaration on the future of the Union*, that 'with ratification of the Treaty of Nice, the European Union will have completed the institutional changes necessary for the accession of new Member

1 The expression executive order is used and analyzed by D. Curtin and M. Egeberg, 'Tradition and innovation: Europe's accumulated executive order', introductory article of the special issue 'Towards a new executive order in Europe?', *West European Politics* 31 (2008) Number 4.

States'.[2] That claim contrasted somewhat with the fact that the very same *Declaration on the future of the Union* launched a new round of public debate on the EU's institutional future which led, one year later, to the decision embodied in the Laeken Declaration to set up a Convention for examining a new and global reform of the founding Treaties. In the Laeken Declaration, the European Council reiterated once more the question that had already been the *leitmotif* of the Amsterdam and Nice intergovernmental conferences, namely 'how we can improve the efficiency of decision-making and the working of the institutions in a Union of some thirty Member States.' The novelty of 'Laeken' was that, in addition to questions relating to the internal operation of the institutions (their composition, their decision-making rules), the relations *between* institutions were given a central place on the new constitutional agenda. For a brief period following the Laeken Declaration, and as the Convention on the Future of the Union started its deliberations, it seemed that everything was up for grabs, and the European Union's institutional system could be the object of a major reform. Pressure for radical change came from the pro-integration camp and was directed at the extension of the so-called Community method across all policy areas of the EU and, linked to this but more daringly, at transforming the European Commission into a true European government whose relation with the Parliament and the Council would become close to the tradition of (bicameral) parliamentary government which most EU Member States are familiar with in their own domestic system.[3] These discussions took place largely outside the framework of the Convention because the Convention's Praesidium had, wisely or not, decided not to create a special Working Group dedicated to the institutions but rather to deal with them at a much later stage of its work, after having absorbed the piecemeal reform proposals dealing with other elements of the European constitutional system. By the time the institutional questions came to the forefront of the Convention debates, in early 2003, the supporters of the *status quo* had reasserted themselves and the idea of a 'grand reform' was shelved. Instead of this, the draft European Constitution proposed to extend the 'Community method' – involving law-making through the codecision procedure – to a number of new policy areas but not to all, thus continuing a cautious and gradual evolution initiated at Maastricht and continued at Amsterdam and Nice. In addition, it proposed some institutional innovations which did not intend to recalibrate the existing balance between Commission, Parliament, Council and European Council, but rather to add some extra elements that would make that existing balance more efficient and democratic (but also more complex!): essentially, a long-term President of the European Council, a Minister for Foreign Affairs belonging to both the Commission and the Council, and a seemingly strengthened role for national parliaments to monitor the EU decision-making process. Those reform proposals were taken on board, with minor changes, by

---

[2] OJ 2001, C 80/85, point 2.

[3] For an academic elaboration of a European institutional model along those lines, see W. Van Gerven, *The European Union – A Polity of States and Peoples* (2005), at pp. 344-368.

the Intergovernmental Conferences that led to the adoption of the Constitutional Treaty in 2004 and its avatar the Treaty of Lisbon in 2007. In this paper, I will not examine those institutional reforms for their own sake, but rather examine whether and to what extent they, together with some less visible treaty amendments, are likely to modify the existing structures for the accountability of executive power in the European Union. In doing so, I will leave aside the new monitoring role for national parliaments which, although principally directed at the Commission, deals with the Union's legislative activity rather than its executive functions.[4] My analysis will be divided in three parts (corresponding to separate sections of this chapter): the accountability issues raised by the institutional innovations in the field of the EU's external relations; the new political control mechanisms resulting from a half-hearted effort to distinguish more sharply between legislative and executive acts; and the more general question of whether the new Treaty text will make EU executive action, and the corresponding accountability lines, more visible than before.

2 New Accountability Problems for EU Foreign Relations

Two institutional 'inventions' mentioned above, namely the creation of a full-time and long-term President of the European Council and the creation of a foreign affairs person combining a Commission and a Council affiliation, are both closely linked to the external relations dimension of the EU system. This is perhaps a surprising result of the Treaty reform process because, in its initial stages, external relations were not a central concern. The Nice Declaration of December 2000 had identified four subjects that required a 'broader debate' (namely: simplification of the treaties, status of the Charter of Rights, delimitation of competences and role of national parliaments), none of which primarily involved the external dimension of EU policies. However, one year later, the Laeken Declaration considerably broadened the constitutional reform agenda and, under the impression of the recent terrorist attack on the United States, the foreign relations of the European Union figured prominently in that document of the European Council. The Declaration contained the oft-cited, and somewhat, trendy, phrase that the EU should 'shoulder its responsibilities in the governance of globalisation'. There was a clearly shared view that the EU should play a more active role on the international scene. That this foreign policy ambition also required further institutional reforms (after the ones made in all previous Treaty revisions) was not altogether obvious, but it quickly became the prevailing wisdom among the members of the Convention on the Future of the Union and was accepted by the governments in the subsequent IGCs.

4 This new legislative accountability mechanism involving national parliaments has already been amply discussed in the literature. See, among others, P. Kiiver, *The National Parliaments in the European Union: A Critical View on EU Constitution-building* (2006); P. Kiiver, 'The Treaty of Lisbon, the national parliaments and the principle of subsidiarity', *Maastricht Journal of European and Comparative Law* 15 (2008) 77-83.

The first notable change is that the Lisbon Treaty increases the formal decision-making role of the European Council in foreign relations, and this role will be boosted by a corresponding increase of its capacity to prepare and implement its decisions through the creation of the post of a long-term *President of the European Council* (new Article 15 of the EU Treaty) who will, quite naturally, seek to maximise the effective application by the other institutions of the European Council's policy indications. So, for example, when trade measures are to be taken, the Commission will preserve its formal right of initiative, but it will have to exercise that right in accordance with the substantive directions given by the European Council, and the new President of the European Council will presumably keep a watchful eye on this.

This increase of the European Council's power is not accompanied by a correction of the traditional constitutional defects of the institution, namely the fact that it does not have any rules of procedure, the fact that it meets behind closed doors and normally decides by unanimity, the fact that it is not subject to European parliamentary control and is subject only to token national parliamentary control, and the fact that the legality of its decisions cannot be directly challenged before the ECJ. So, whereas the Lisbon Treaty grants new control powers to the European Council over the Commission and the Council, it fails to organise any kind of improved accountability for the European Council itself, or indeed for its new long-term President except that (s)he will present a report of European Council meetings to the European Parliament – but this is already done today by the rotating Presidency of the Council.

One of the most widely trumpeted achievements of the Convention and the Constitutional Treaty was the creation of the double-hat figure of the *Union Minister for Foreign Affairs* – which aimed at putting an end to the embarrassingly overlapping roles of a variety of EU foreign policy actors. The Lisbon Treaty cancelled the new denomination, as part of its 'constitution- eradication' approach, and reverted to the traditional denomination of High Representative.[5] However, this was only a terminological change which did not affect the definition of the role of this institutional figure, as it had been spelled out in the Constitutional Treaty. Under the rules of the Lisbon Treaty (new Article 18 EU Treaty), the 'post-Solana' High Representative will act both as the Chair of the Foreign Affairs Council (replacing, in this role, the minister from the country holding the rotating Presidency of the EU) and as a Vice-President of the Commission in charge of external relations. This spectacular reform, creating a 'personal bridge' between the Commission and the Council, had been recommended by Working Group VII of the Convention on the future of

[5] European Council of June 2007, Conclusions of the Presidency, Annex 1, para.3 : 'The TEU and the Treaty on the Functioning of the Union will not have a constitutional character. The terminology used throughout the Treaties will reflect this change: the term 'Constitution' will not be used, the 'Union Minister for Foreign Affairs' will be called High Representative of the Union for Foreign Affairs and Security Policy....'.

the Union in its final report[6] and had been eagerly approved by the plenary of the Convention. It became the central institutional innovation proposed by the Convention, and can be seen as part of an attempt to smoothen the remaining differences between the supranational and the intergovernmental dimensions of external relations in a formally de-pillarized Treaty structure.[7] The members of the Convention seemed particularly proud of this institutional innovation and, in fact, both the Commission and the European Parliament, in their opinions for the subsequent IGC, listed this proposal among the most positive achievements of the Convention and expressed their confidence that it would improve the effectiveness of the EU's foreign policy and its visibility at home and in the wider world.

However, as time went by since this innovation was originally put forward, and even before it has become a living reality, more critical opinions were increasingly expressed. The scepticism relates on the one hand to the capacity of one single person (be it assisted by competent staff) to keep a large number of foreign policy balls in the air simultaneously, and on the other hand (more directly relevant to the theme of this paper) to the serious accountability conflicts that are inscribed in the function. Under the current rules, the High Representative is an emanation of the Council and exclusively accountable to it. Under the new rules, the High Representative will occasionally be torn apart between his/her role as member of the Commission (subject, among other things, to collegial decision-making) and his/her complex role as both the chairperson of the Council and the executive arm of decisions of the Council and European Council. Depending on the way the High Representative will deal with these constraints and divergent institutional rules, there may be a creeping expansion of the Commission's role in CFSP, or on the contrary a greater overall control of the (European) Council and the Member States on that part of external relations which falls currently within the scope of the first pillar (trade, development, environment, immigration, etc.).[8] Such gradual shifts have occurred ever since the Treaty of Maastricht erected the pillars, but the creation of a pivotal High Representative might blur the lines of the horizontal division of powers between the EU institutions to a much greater extent than

---

6 Working Group VII 'External Action', Final report of 16 December 2002, CONV 459/02, p. 5. The Working Group had discussed various alternative options; see the reflection of that discussion at pp. 19-23 of its report. A 'large trend' (p. 23) emerged in favour of the double-hat figure, for which the Working Group proposed the name 'European External Representative' (later modified in the Praesidium's draft articles into 'Union Minister for Foreign Affairs').

7 The story of the 'invention' of the Foreign Affairs Minister by the Convention is told by G. Grevi, 'The institutional framework of external action', in: G. Amato, H. Bribosia, B. De Witte (eds), *Genesis and Destiny of the European Constitution* (2007) 773-805, and by J. De Ruyt, 'A minister for a European foreign policy', *EUI – RSCAS Policy Papers* 2005/03.

8 See J. Wouters, 'The Union Minister for Foreign Affairs: Europe's single voice or Trojan horse?', in: J.W. de Zwaan et al., *The European Union: An Ongoing Process of Integration – Liber Amicorum Alfred E. Kellermann* (2004) 77-86.

before. Even assuming that such shifts will not occur and that the High Representative will indeed manage to juggle both roles and walk the bi-institutional tightrope as a perfect 'Mr Check and Balance', there will nevertheless be an unprecedented concentration in the hands of one person of a variety of policy determination and policy execution functions.[9] This concentration of power sits uneasily with the traditional institutional balance system of the EC, whereby the institutions control and counterbalance each other's actions. The hypothesis that the High Representative could develop into an autonomous power centre, escaping from any effective control by the institutions, is made more plausible by the fact that (s)he will, according to the new Treaty rules (Article 27, para. 3 TEU), have the support of a newly created European External Action Service, grouping officials of the Commission and the Council, as well as staff seconded from the national diplomatic services. Alternatively, one could fear that the High Representative will be over-accountable. On the basis of the Treaty rules, (s)he would have a relationship of accountability to no less than four other actors: the President of the Commission, the European Parliament (as control organ of the Commission), the Council and the European Council (represented now by its own President).

3 The New but Incomplete Typology of Executive Acts

Less visible than the creation of new institutional actors is the partial reform, hidden in the far corners of the Treaty on the Functioning of the Union, of the system of EU legal instruments. That reform is less radical than what had been envisaged under the Constitutional Treaty, which aimed at abolishing the current 'directive', at transforming the current 'regulation', and at introducing the new instruments called 'law' and 'framework law'. This part of the reform was undone by the Lisbon Treaty, so that directives and regulations will survive in their current form and with their current roles. However, some other aspects of the reform have survived the downsizing of the Constitutional Treaty and they may affect to some extent the current accountability structures of EU activity.

The main novelty of the post-Lisbon regime is the creation of a new intermediate level of law-making, between the purely legislative and purely executive, namely the *delegated acts* (Article 290 TFU). These will be adopted by the Commission in order to 'supplement or amend certain non-essential elements of the legislative acts.' In contrast with implementing acts, such delegated acts may, thus, actually modify a legislative act, albeit only on non-essential points. They will be allowed only if a specific delegation is made within the relevant legislative act, and they will subject to control by the institutions that have adopted that act (normally speaking, the Council and the Parliament). When

9 S. Griller, 'External relations', in: B. de Witte (ed), *Ten Reflections on the Constitutional Treaty for Europe* (2003) 133-161, at pp. 146-7.

envisaging the implications of this Lisbon Treaty provision, one must remember that the practice whereby the Commission is given the power to amend or supplement legislative acts exists already today, but this practice is considered to be covered by the Commission's general implementation powers and has no explicit Treaty basis.[10] So, under the current system, there was for a long time no need to sharply distinguish between 'amending or supplementing measures' and 'implementing measures', since the decision-making mechanism was identical for both types of measures. Moreover, that distinction is often arduous, particularly in the case of broad framework legislation.[11] However, the disadvantage of this lack of differentiation in the current system is that, to use the words of the Convention Working Group's final report, 'the legislator is obliged either to go into minute detail in the provisions it adopts, or to entrust to the Commission the more technical or detailed aspects of the legislation as if they were implementing measures.'[12]

In reality, the dilemma is not as stark as the Working Group report puts it, because the existence of the comitology system means that the detailed aspects are 'entrusted' to the Commission, yes, but subject to an external check on what it purports to do. That check was traditionally exercised by the Council and not by the other branch of the legislative power, the EP. However, in 2006, a new comitology procedure was added to the three existing ones, namely the so-called regulatory procedure with scrutiny. This applies to cases in which a committee considers Commission drafts for amendment of non-essential parts of EC legislation which was adopted under co-decision: since such Commission measures can be considered as quasi-legislative acts (they involve actual changes, albeit of a technical nature, of EC legislation), rather than mere implementation, it was thought proper to allow each of the two legislative organs, the Council and the European Parliament, to scrutinize and actually overturn an opinion of the committee involved.[13] This mechanism partially prefigures the control mecha-

10 See J-Cl. Piris, *The Constitution for Europe: A Legal Analysis* (2006) at p. 73: 'Practice to date under the expression "implementing powers" has combined two types of power which are different in nature: the power to adopt a normative act which amends or supplements the basic legislative act itself, on the one hand, and the power to implement, or to execute at EC level, all or part of a legislative act, on the other hand.'

11 See for example the Directive of 3 December 2001 on general product safety (OJ 2002, L 11/4). It does not contain substantive safety standards itself, but leaves it to the European Commission to set safety requirements for particular products, which are then to be implemented by private standardisation bodies. One recent example is the Commission Decision of 25 March 2008 on the fire safety requirements to be met by European standards for cigarettes (OJ 2008, L 83/35). Is this a measure which 'supplements' or only 'implements' the Directive?

12 Convention on the Future of the Union, Final report of Working Group IX on Simplification, 29 November 2002, CONV 42/02, at p. 8.

13 Council Decision 2006/512 amending Decision 1999/468, of 17 July 2006, OJ 2006, L 200/11. See, for an analysis of the negotiation process and content of this reform, G. Schusterschitz and S. Kotz, 'The comitology reform of 2006 – increasing the powers of the European Parliament without changing the

nism which the new Treaty will require for delegated acts. So, seen from this perspective, the new category of delegated acts does not come out of the blue, but is rather the latest development in a long-standing bargaining process between the EU institutions on where to draw the line between the role of the legislative and the executive, and on how to organize oversight by the legislator on acts adopted by the executive.[14] It remains to be seen, in actual practice, whether the creation of a formal distinction between delegated acts and 'pure' implementing acts will add to the transparency and accountability of EU decision-making, and how it will affect the power relations between the EU institutions.

Delegated acts and implementing acts will both be adopted by the Commission, according to its own internal decision-making rules, but the distinction will be relevant in terms of the control mechanisms imposed on the Commission when it enacts such measures. In the case of implementing acts, the Commission's power will remain subject to the current comitology system, or rather a variation thereof that will be adopted after the entry into force of the Lisbon Treaty.[15] In the case of delegated acts, the Commission will be subject to a new and stricter control mechanism which, according to the new Article 290 TFEU, will either allow the European Parliament or the Council to revoke the delegation; or permit the entry into force of the delegated act only if Parliament or Council have not objected against it within a given period of time. The precise terms of these new control mechanisms need to be worked out further once the Lisbon Treaty is in force, perhaps by means of an inter-institutional agreement.

The preceding observations may convey the impression that the Lisbon Treaty introduces a tight three-level structure of law-making (legislation, delegated acts, implementing acts), each with its own mechanism of political accountability. But that impression is misleading because we find, lurking in the folds of the Lisbon Treaty, decision-making mechanisms (and, hence, accountability lines) that do not fit in the three-level structure. First, we read in Article 24(1) TEU that both the Council and the European Council will have the power to adopt decisions in the field of Common Foreign and Security Policy, but that

Treaties', *European Constitutional Law Review* 3 (2007) 68-90; and K. Bradley, 'Halfway house: the 2006 comitology reforms and the European Parliament', *West European Politics* 31 (2008) 837-864.

14 It is worth noting, though, that this evolution took the form, most of the time, of interstitial change in between Treaty revision rounds, whereas this time a change is entrenched through formal treaty amendment. See, on the earlier evolution process, C.-F. Bergström, H. Farrell and A. Héritier, 'Legislate or delegate? Bargaining over implementation and legislative authority in the EU', *West European Politics* 30 (2007), 338-366.

15 See Article 291(3) TFEU. The fact that the existing comitology mechanism must be revised after the entry into force of the Treaty of Lisbon is not expressly mentioned, but results implicitly from the text of the Article where it states that the control mechanism must be adopted 'by means of regulations in accordance with the ordinary legislative procedure', whereas currently the mechanism is laid down in decisions adopted by the Council alone. So, the current comitology decision (as last revised in 2006) will have to be modified in order to allow the European Parliament to exercise its new co-decision powers in this respect (and in order to transform it into a regulation).

'the adoption of legislative acts shall be excluded'. So, we will have binding legal instruments that are not legislative acts, but are not delegated or implementing measures either, since they will be based directly on the Treaty. In other words, these acts do not fit in the hierarchical three-level model sketched above, but will have a separate existence outside this hierarchy. During the Convention and the two IGCs leading up to the Treaty of Lisbon, they were often referred to as 'autonomous acts', in analogy with the *règlements autonomes* in French constitutional law.[16] This is not just a specific feature, among many others, of the CFSP sub-system. More surprisingly, we will find the same phenomenon in more traditional areas of EU law, where we will see, under the Lisbon Treaty, binding legal acts that are not legislative acts although they very much look like them. For example, in the field of competition law, Article 103 TFEU states that 'the appropriate regulations and directives to give effect to the principles set out in Articles 101 and 102 shall be laid down by the Council, on a proposal from the Commission and after consulting the European Parliament.'[17] What is referred to here are acts such as Regulation 1/2003 on the modernisation of competition law, which is a legislative measure by any standard meaning of that term; and yet, Article 103 does not say that these acts will have to be made either through the ordinary or through a special legislative procedure, and therefore they will not be 'legislative acts' in the sense of the Lisbon Treaty![18] This qualification as non-legislative acts seems arbitrary.[19] The same is true for Council acts setting out general rules in the field of state aid (Article 109 TFEU), and there are a number of other cases.[20] The fact that we will have important binding instruments, in traditional fields of EU law, that will be neither legislative nor execu-

16 J. Ziller, 'National constitutional concepts in the new Constitution for Europe. Part two', *European Constitutional Law Review* 1 (2005) 452-480, at p. 469.

17 These are the Treaty articles laying down the substantive principles of competition law, corresponding to the current Articles 81 and 82 EC Treaty.

18 Indeed, the Lisbon Treaty sets forth a procedural definition of legislative acts. Legislative acts are those that are adopted in accordance with a procedure which is defined (in the relevant Treaty base) as either the ordinary legislative procedure (i.e. codecision) or a specific legislative procedure. See Article 289, para. 3 TFEU.

19 See the criticism by M. Dougan, 'The Treaty of Lisbon 2007: winning minds, not hearts', *Common Market Law Review* 45 (2008) 617-703, at p. 647.

20 In his analysis of the Constitutional Treaty, Stancanelli lists 76 legal bases for non-legislative acts of the Council, and 17 for the European Council. However, this list includes a number of organisational measures, appointments, etc., which do not have a law-making character (P. Stancanelli, 'Le système décisionnel de l'Union', in: G. Amato, H. Bribosia, B. De Witte (eds), *Genesis and Destiny of the European Constitution* (2007) 485-543, at p. 532-534). If one excludes those, there are still 19 cases where binding non-legislative acts can be adopted directly on the basis of the Treaties; see the list in E. Best, 'Legislative procedures after Lisbon: fewer, simpler, clearer?', *Maastricht Journal of European and Comparative Law* 15 (2008) 85-96, at p. 94.

tive, formally speaking, makes a bit of a mockery of an otherwise careful effort to establish a distinction between legislative and executive acts of EU law.[21]

This 'incomplete hierarchy' is not just an aesthetic failing of the simplification effort. Practical legal consequences will flow from the identification of an act as being legislative, executive or neither of the two. One consequence is the existence or not of an obligation for the Council to deliberate in public; this obligation will only apply to legislative acts[22], and therefore the scope of this obligation will be narrower than today when the Council's Rules of Procedure provide for public deliberation (subject to exceptions) for a more broadly defined category of legislative acts which includes, among others, Council acts in the field of competition and state aid.[23] Another practical consequence relates to the new role of national parliaments in monitoring respect for the principle of subsidiarity. This role is limited to draft legislative acts only and will therefore not apply to the *règlements autonomes*.[24] Finally, the distinction may possibly be relevant to the new definition of the individual right to challenge EU acts directly before the European Court: it will apply to 'regulatory acts' which do not require further implementing measures,[25] but this term is not further defined. It presumably does not cover legislative acts, but does it cover autonomous non-legislative acts such as those mentioned above? We cannot know this from the text of the Treaty. This is a case of very sloppy treaty drafting, which remained in place all the way from the original draft Constitutional Treaty proposed by the Convention until the Lisbon Treaty.

4 Greater Visibility of EU Executive Power?

Contrary to the EU legislative and judicial institutions, which are described in some detail, the EU's executive power is only alluded to in the current text of the founding Treaties. Whereas one can deduce from the Treaty text that both the Commission and the Council possess executive powers, these powers are described in provisions scattered all over the EC and EU Treaties, and there is no comprehensive description of the EU executive power as such. The important reality of comitology is referred to in Article 202 EC Treaty but

[21] Paolo Stancanelli describes it more gently (n. 20 above, at p. 517): *'une exception de taille à l'articulation rigoureuse entre la fonction législative et la fonction exécutive.'*

[22] New Article 16(8) TEU.

[23] A point noted by J.B. Liisberg, 'The EU Constitutional Treaty and its distinction between legislative and non-legislative acts', in: B. Egelund Olsen, K. Engsig Sørensen (eds), *Regulation in the EU* (2006) 133-168, at p. 161. The current regime of Council publicity is outlined in Article 8 of the Council's Rules of Procedure as last amended by Council Decision of 15 September 2006, OJ 2006, L 285/47. See, on the background and significance of the latest reform in 2006, M.E. de Leeuw, 'Openness in the legislative process in the European Union', *European Law Review* (2007) 295-318.

[24] See the text of the Protocol on the application of the principles of subsidiarity and proportionality.

[25] New Article 263 TFEU.

not really described. Particular modes of executive action that differ from the traditional treaty-based modes (for example, the open method of coordination) are provided for particular policy areas (such as employment, see Article 128 EC Treaty) but not for other areas in which they are also used nowadays. Agencies that act as additional executive bodies separate from the Commission and the Council have mushroomed in recent years, but are not mentioned in the Treaties either.

The promoters and drafters of the Constitutional Treaty had the ambition of codifying existing institutional arrangements so as to make them more visible, so that one could have expected the Constitutional Treaty (and Lisbon Treaty) to present a more coherent picture of EU executive action and, related to that, of the accountability lines relating to that executive action. In reality, this has happened only to a very limited extent.

The Lisbon Treaty, following on the footsteps of the Constitutional Treaty, does make a valiant effort to present a concise and comprehensible view of the main functions of each of the principal EU institutions. In doing so, however, it remains rather reluctant to use the term 'executive'. For example, the first sentences of Article 17 TEU correctly describe the main constitutional functions of the *Commission*, and then the next sentence adds: 'It shall exercise coordinating, executive and management functions, as laid down by the Treaties.' It is not clear whether this phrase is meant to summarize the nature of the specific functions listed in the previous sentences, or refers to something additional. It is also not clear which difference, if any, the authors of the Treaty saw between 'executive' and 'coordinating' or 'management' functions. In respect of the *Council*, the corresponding Article 16 TEU does not use the term 'executive' at all, although it becomes clear from reading the text that the Council is, and remains, an important executive actor alongside the Commission. The same applies to the *European Council* whose role (and that of its President) is abundantly described in Article 15 TEU but without using the word 'executive', although one could say, in this case, that the executive nature of the European Council is imprinted on it by the sentence stating that it 'shall not exercise legislative functions'(Article 15, para 1 TEU).

Whereas the Convention and the two IGCs have spent much effort in defining the roles of the main executive actors and of their direct emanations, such as the President of the European Council and the High Representative for Foreign Affairs, they have paid much less attention to the executive 'undergrowth'[26] consisting of the EU's satellite bodies and the new modes of governance. In this respect, the two revision Treaties of 2004 and 2007 are documents of traditional constitutionalism, paying little or no attention to experimental governance. There has been no serious attempt to codify the main rules for the establishment of agencies and their own decision-making, despite the fact that these have become increasingly important parts of the EU administration. The unin-

[26] An expression used by D. Curtin, 'Holding (quasi-)autonomous EU administrative actors to public account', *European Law Journal* 3 (2007) 523-541, at p. 540.

formed reader cannot guess, from reading the founding Treaties as amended by the Lisbon Treaty, that agencies have become important executive actors in the present-day European Union. Some specific agencies are mentioned in the Treaty text,[27] but they are nowhere mentioned as a category and the decision-making and accountability mechanisms of most of them will still be dealt with in an ad-hoc manner without any overarching principles laid down in the Treaty.[28]

There has been, in the past decade, an upsurge of academic interest and effective use of what is generally termed the *open method of coordination* (OMC), although in reality this term hides a number of individual methods that are partially different in each relevant policy area, including employment, macro-economic policy, social exclusion and education, to name but a few.[29] The term open method of coordination, which was coined by the Lisbon European Council in 2000, does not figure in the current text of the Treaties, but the Laeken declaration referred to it, and the Convention's Working Group on simplification recommended that 'constitutional status should be assigned to the open method of coordination, which involves concerted action by the Member States outside the competences attributed to the Union by the treaties.'[30] This sentence expresses a curious miscomprehension of the OMC (it is clearly not used outside but *inside* the EU's competences), which is symptomatic of the lack of sustained attention accorded to it by the Convention. In the end, and despite calls from academics,[31] the Convention decided not to give a comprehensive constitutional status to the OMC, but rather, by way of compromise, a description of a method of action which corresponds to the OMC – but without using the term – was included in the Treaty articles dealing with the policy areas of public health, industry and research.[32] In addition, the existing, and differently formulated references to policy coordination were kept for the areas of economic union and employment. This fragmented and unsatisfactory approach was maintained in the Lisbon Treaty[33] so that the question inevitably arises: given that the Lisbon

---

27 See Article 45 TEU (European Defence Agency) and Article 88 TFEU (European Police Office).

28 For discussion of the current accountability structures of EU agencies, see D. Curtin, n. 26 above, and P. Craig, *EU Administrative Law* (2006), at pp. 164-182.

29 The very rich literature describing the various forms taken by the OMC includes: K. Armstrong and C. Kilpatrick, 'Law, Governance, or New Governance? The Changing Open Method of Coordination', *Columbia Journal of European Law* 13 (2007) 649-677; E. Szyszczak, 'Experimental Governance: The Open Method of Coordination', *European Law Journal* 12 (2006) 486-502.

30 Final report of Working Group IX on Simplification, 29 November 2002, CONV 42/02, p. 7.

31 See G. de Búrca and J. Zeitlin, 'Constitutionalising the Open Method of Coordination: A Note for the Convention', *CEPS Policy Brief*, no. 31, March 2003.

32 For a survey of the Convention debate on whether to 'constitutionalize' the OMC, see M. Tsakatika, 'The open method of coordination in the European Convention – An opportunity lost?', in: L. Dobson and A. Follesdal (eds), *Political Theory and the European Convention* (2004) 91-102.

33 The three identically phrased references to the method, in relation to public health, industry and research, can be found in Articles 168, 173 and 181 TFEU.

Treaty formally recognises the use of the method in certain areas, does this mean that it may not be used in other policy areas where it is currently used (such as education) or where it might be used in the future (such as immigration)? In sum, the Lisbon Treaty does not much clarify the legal status, and availability, of the open method of coordination. Consequently, it does not deal either with the very real accountability concerns, and other normative concerns, which the use of OMC raises.[34]

34 For a discussion of those issues, see A. Benz, 'Accountable multilevel governance by the open method of coordination?', *European Law Journal* 13 (2007) 505-522.

CHAPTER 14

Executive Accountability and the Contestability of the Executive Domain

Paul Craig

This chapter does not purport to provide some magic solution to the enduring problems concerning executive accountability, whether in national law or EU law. There is a wealth of literature on such issues, which must necessarily be addressed against the background of the specific political system in question and against the background of the particular type of executive function. The objective of this chapter is more modest, but it does nonetheless seek to link three issues that are related, albeit not often considered together.

The first is whether a particular function should be regarded as an executive function at all. Or to put the same point in a different manner, to inquire in what sense the phrase executive function is being used when an institution claims to be the repository of that function. It will be seen in the course of the following analysis that while certain functions are generally agreed to inhere in the executive, there is considerably more contestability as to whether this should be so in relation to other functions.

The second issue is premised on an affirmative answer to the first inquiry, in the sense that it is accepted that a particular function is properly regarded as residing with the executive branch of government. This still then leaves open the identification of the executive. This will normally not be problematic in the classic Westphalian state, since the executive will paradigmatically be comprised of the government led by a prime minister or president. There are nonetheless more difficult issues concerning the boundaries of the executive, even within traditional nation states, as exemplified by the proliferation of agencies, contracting-out and the like. These problems are even more pronounced in a polity such as the EU where executive power does not reside within a single institution, but is rather shared between the Commission, the European Council, the Council and agencies.

The third issue concerns the optimal way of structuring accountability for the exercise of the particular executive function. This inquiry is premised on an affirmative answer to the first inquiry, and some resolution of the second inquiry: it is accepted after proper reflection that a particular function is properly regarded as residing with the executive branch of government, and the particular branch of the executive has been duly identified. The optimal method of securing executive accountability will then depend on the particular executive function that is being performed. Generalizations as to the optimal meaning of executive accountability are perforce of limited utility, even more so given the increasingly complex way in which executive functions are organized in the modern nation state and within the EU. The precise blend of legal, political and financial controls will need to be tailored to the specific executive function under examination.

It would clearly not be possible to apply this three-step methodology to all species of actual or alleged executive power within nation states and the EU. That would require a book in itself, or perhaps a whole life's work. The discussion that follows will therefore seek to exemplify this methodology, in relation to certain allegedly executive functions within one nation state, the UK, and the

EU. This discussion will however be framed by more general consideration of the three issues set out above, which draws on experience from a broader range of polities.

1 The UK

(a) The Delineation and Contestability of Executive Functions

(i) General Precepts

The delineation of executive functions and the powers that flow from them has always been problematic and contestable.

Formal constitutions provide relatively little assistance in this regard. The inadequacy of formal, constitutional definitions of executive power is a widely shared phenomenon. There are gaps and silences in the constitutions of countries as diverse as the USA, Australia, Canada, New Zealand, Scotland, France and even Germany.[1] It is moreover relatively rare to find a complete enumeration of executive powers within modern polities. This is frequently done in relation to legislative powers, more especially where they are federally divided, such as in the USA or Australia. Such specification of legislative power is also evident in relation to the devolved powers of Scotland, in relation to which the Scotland Act 1998 lists in great detail the legislative powers reserved to the Westminster parliament. The federal division of executive power does not however necessarily follow the federal division of legislative power. Constitutionally enumerated lists of law-making powers are a misleading guide to the location of executive power. Formal constitutions therefore offer very imperfect or incomplete guidance as to the delineation of executive power.

Different nation states adopt differing approaches to the delimitation of executive power.[2] The 'subordinate' approach conceives of the executive as the agent of the legislature, or in some instances as agent of the general will of the sovereign people.

The 'bits and pieces' approach sees the boundaries of executive power being set not by any governing principle, but by the pragmatic choices of the legislature. On this view the most significant source of executive power is legislation and this is so notwithstanding the existence of non-statutory executive power in the form of executive privilege or prerogative power. As such, the boundaries of executive power are for the most part set by the extent to which parliaments pass laws that confer powers on the government. On this approach the delimitation of executive power is less a matter of constitutional principle than it is the result of practical politics.

---

1 P. Craig and A. Tomkins, 'Introduction', in P. Craig and A. Tomkins (eds), *The Executive and Public Law, Power and Accountability in Comparative Perspective* (Oxford University Press, 2006).

2 Ibid 6-8.

The 'residual' approach sees executive power as that power which is not exercised by anyone else. It is what is left over. On this view executive power is perceived in negative terms, being that which is neither legislative, nor judicial.

It might be felt that greater specificity as to the delineation of 'executive function' could be reached by focusing on the meaning of this phrase. It is true that in one sense the very concept of executive function connotes the 'implementation', 'execution' or 'putting into effect' of rules that will normally have been devised by the legislature. This concept of the executive function, which is broadly shared by most polities, is nonetheless fraught with difficulty on closer examination, since it leaves open to question whether the executive should merely have the power of implementation stricto sensu, or whether it should also be regarded as within the sphere of the executive to devise secondary rules that will put into effect the principles contained in the primary legislation. It should moreover be acknowledged that other functions have commonly been regarded as within the executive's sphere in the UK and other countries that have little to do with 'execution' in this sense. Thus the maintenance of internal order, foreign policy, defence of the state, and the formulation of legislative policy are commonly regarded as being within the remit of the executive, although it should be recognized that merely because a particular function has been felt properly to fall within the sphere of the executive, this does not in itself indicate the particular powers that should be accorded to the executive to fulfil that function.

(ii) Prerogative Power in the UK

The contestability as to the delineation of executive power is exemplified by recent developments in the UK concerning prerogative power.

Such power has traditionally been regarded as inhering in the executive. It originated or emanated from the Crown in his or her personal capacity, but in the modern day most prerogative powers are exercised by the Prime Minister or other ministers in the name of the Crown, hence the appellation royal prerogative. Accountability was secured through legal and political means.[3]

The courts would control the existence and extent of prerogative power, but not the manner of exercise. They would adjudicate on whether a prerogative power existed and if the answer was affirmative the courts would then determine its extent. They did not however assert jurisdiction to control the manner of exercise of an admitted prerogative power until the twentieth century in the landmark *GCHQ* case, in which the courts held that, subject to limited qualifications, the normal controls of judicial review were applicable to prerogative discretionary power as well as statutory discretionary power.[4]

The manner of exercise of admitted prerogative was however increasingly controlled politically by Parliament in the eighteenth and nineteenth centuries.

---

3 P. Craig, 'Prerogative, Precedent and Power', in: C. Forsyth and I. Hare (eds), *The Golden Metwand and the Crooked Cord, Essays in Honour of Sir William Wade* (Oxford University Press, 1998), 65-91.

4 *Council of Civil Service Unions v Minister for the Civil Service* [1985] AC 374, 410-411.

The prerogative powers which were of principal importance during this period were those of ministerial appointment and the dissolution of Parliament. These were the main powers through which the King could maintain control over Parliament. In the seventeenth and eighteenth centuries Parliament sought, both directly and indirectly, to constrain these prerogative powers. The point being made here can be put in another way. Whereas the judiciary focused on placing limits to the *existence* or *extent* of prerogative power, Parliament sought not only to do this, but also to limit the *manner of exercise* of this species of power.

However notwithstanding these legal and political controls designed to enhance accountability over executive prerogative power, the basic precept remained unchallenged, this being that such power did reside with the executive. The very rationale for the ascription of this power to the executive was not always self-evident and at the very least the reasons were eclectic; no single rationale could serve to explain or justify in normative terms the ascription of this degree of power to the executive. This is readily apparent when one considers the list of such prerogative powers.

The Government exercises prerogative powers to: deploy and use the Armed Forces overseas; make and ratify treaties; issue, refuse, impound and revoke passports; acquire and cede territory; dissolve Parliament; conduct diplomacy; send and receive ambassadors; organize the Civil Service. The Government moreover makes recommendations to the Monarch to exercise her powers to: grant honours or decorations; grant mercy; grant peerages; and appoint Ministers.

The rationale for why such powers should be thought to inhere in the executive is, as stated above, by no means self-evident and it is clear that the same rationale cannot serve to explain all such instances of prerogative power. Thus in some instances the primary rationale, as exemplified by deployment of forces overseas, and the conduct of diplomacy appears to be the need for the executive to take action without securing the approval of Parliament, hence the acceptance that the executive has non-statutory discretionary power over such matters in the form of prerogative power. This rationale however clearly does not serve to explain the prerogative power to dissolve Parliament whenever the government so wishes. Nor does it explain the prerogative power to organize the civil service. The full force of this latter power should moreover be recognized. It not only allows the executive to rearrange the ministries of government. It also enables the government to engage in fundamental re-thinking of the way in which the entirety of government services are organized, as exemplified by the sweeping changes in the pattern of executive governance in the UK from the 1980s onwards, whereby we witnessed the division between policy making preserved in traditional departments of government and policy execution hived off to what are now termed executive agencies, all of which was done without any statutory foundation, or legislative sanction.

It is therefore interesting and timely that the Brown Government in the UK has recently signalled a willingness to reassess whether these powers should inhere in the executive. The Governance of Britain Paper July 2007 is central in this respect.[5] The Green Paper addressed a number of issues relating to executive accountability, including whether the executive should continue to have the prerogative powers traditionally vested in it. The Green Paper signalled a change of thinking in this respect, whereby the government would accept greater controls over such powers. The relevant passages are as follows.

> 14. For centuries the executive has, in certain areas, been able to exercise authority in the name of the Monarch without the people and their elected representatives in their Parliament being consulted. This is no longer appropriate in a modern democracy. The Government believes that the executive should draw its powers from the people, through Parliament.
>
> 15. The flow of power from the people to government should be balanced by the ability of Parliament to hold government to account. However, when the executive relies on the powers of the royal prerogative – powers where government acts upon the Monarch's authority – it is difficult for Parliament to scrutinise and challenge government's actions. If voters do not believe that government wields its power appropriately or that it is properly accountable then public confidence in the accountability of decision-making risks being lost.
>
> 16. That is why the Government is proposing immediate and specific changes to strengthen our democracy – changes that will restrict the power of the Prime Minister and the executive.
>
> 17. It is important that the key decisions that affect the whole country – such as the decision to send troops into armed conflict – are made in the right way, and with Parliament's consent. The same is true of treaties that the UK makes with its partners in Europe and across the world. Government's power to deploy troops and ratify treaties stems from the royal prerogative. In a modern 21st century parliamentary democracy, the Government considers that basing these powers on the prerogative is out of date. It will therefore seek to limit its own power by placing the most important of these prerogative powers onto a more formal footing, conferring power on Parliament to determine how they are exercised in future. And where archaic powers are no longer in use – for example the right to impress people into the Royal Navy – the Government will consider options for ending them.
>
> 18. Recent years have seen increased concern about the security of the nation and additional measures to protect people and their livelihoods. Decisions about our national security affect us all and it is important to look at how the scrutiny of intelligence and security matters can become more transparent in a way that strengthens the legitimacy of, and support for, our security and intelligence Agencies without putting our collective safety at risk.

5 *Governance of Britain*, Cm 7170 (2007).

> 19. It is important that Parliament is strengthened to ensure that its own powers – whether ancient or more recently acquired – continue to be exercised effectively within appropriate limits and in a way that means the people whom it serves understand its work and have faith in its decisions.
>
> Moving royal prerogative powers to Parliament
>
> 20. In most modern democracies, the government's only powers are those granted to it by a written constitution or by the legislature. A distinguishing feature of the British constitution is the extent to which government continues to exercise a number of powers which were not granted to it by a written constitution, nor by Parliament, but are, rather, ancient prerogatives of the Crown. These powers derive from arrangements which preceded the 1689 Declaration of Rights and have been accumulated by the government without Parliament or the people having a say.
>
> 21. The powers acquired by government in this way are commonly referred to as the "royal prerogative" powers but this term includes a number of powers, not all of which are exercised by the government [...]
>
> [...].
>
> 23. The prerogative powers of the Government cannot be exercised without restraint. The 1689 Bill of Rights formally curtailed the powers of the Crown by legislating to remove or outlaw a number of ancient rights of the Crown and subsequent statutes and conventions have limited them further. Moreover, the courts scrutinise the exercise of many of the powers through the mechanism of judicial review, whereby the actions of a Minister can be challenged on the basis that he or she did not have the power to act in such a way, or that the act was unreasonable. Ultimately Ministers are also accountable to Parliament for their actions in exercising the prerogative powers. Ministers can be required to answer questions on any decisions they take, or on any policies they introduce, regardless of whether Parliament or the prerogative has conferred on them the power to act.
>
> 24. The Government believes that in general the prerogative powers should be put onto a statutory basis and brought under stronger parliamentary scrutiny and control. This will ensure that government is more clearly subject to the mandate of the peoples' representatives.

The Green Paper then considered in more detail the ways in which the principal prerogative powers exercised by the executive should be reformed in order that they could be subject to the proper sphere degree of parliamentary control. The government's thinking in this respect has been taken forward by the White Paper on *Constitutional Renewal*,[6] which contains more concrete proposals for the reform of certain prerogative powers. Thus it is proposed to formalize the procedure for Parliament to scrutinize treaties prior to ratification to ensure that a treaty cannot be ratified unless a copy of it is laid before Parliament for a defined period of 21 sitting days. The Government proposes to place the Civil

6 *The Governance of Britain, Constitutional Renewal*, Cm 7342 (2008).

Service on a statutory footing by enshrining in statute the core values of the Civil Service and placing the Civil Service Commissioners on statutory footing. The Government also proposes in relation to war powers that there should be a House of Commons resolution which sets out in detail the processes Parliament should follow in order to approve any commitment of armed forces into armed conflict; the resolution will define a clear role for Parliament, while ensuring that national security is not compromised. A draft Constitutional Renewal Bill is under consideration that will bring these changes into effect.

It is not the purpose of this paper to comment in detail on these proposed changes, or others that might flow from this recent reform exercise. It is rather to exemplify the proposition made at the outset concerning the contestability of executive power. The recent reform exercises in the UK are to be welcomed insofar as they exhibit a willingness on the part of the government to reconsider preexisting orthodoxy, even when this entails some diminution of its own powers. The functions regarded as inhering in the executive should not be seen as fixed or ossified. We should be willing to question whether there are good practical and/or normative arguments for the retention of such power by the executive, and make changes accordingly. This is more especially so given that a number of factors have served to augment national executive power, such as membership of the EU.

(b) The Identification of the Executive

If the delineation of executive power can be contestable, the institutions that are regarded as falling within the executive can also be problematic. The public law regimes of many of nation states have struggled to develop accounts of executive authority that match the structural complexity of modern executive power. Both executive functions and institutions have undergone considerable change in recent years and public law has often laboured to keep up.

This has been a prominent feature of developments in the UK.[7] The revolution in the pattern of government began in earnest in the 1980s under Thatcher. Until then the civil service was still cast in the mould set by the Northcote-Trevelyan reforms of the mid-nineteenth century. It was a unified and uniform service in theory at least, and in most instances in reality too. Governmental functions were organised in and through departments. This was in contrast with the pattern of administration in the earlier part of the nineteenth century when public functions were often undertaken by boards, which operated outside the confines of departments. The latter part of the nineteenth century witnessed the decline in such institutions and the emergence of ministerial responsibility, with the corollary of civil service anonymity.

7 P. Craig, *Administrative Law* (Sweet & Maxwell, 6th ed, 2008), Chap 4.

By the 1960s strains had begun to appear in this organizational structure. These became apparent in the Report of the *Fulton Committee*.[8] It stressed the need for improved efficiency within traditional departments, and pressed for reassessment of the activities required to be undertaken directly within the department. Many activities might work better if they were 'hived off' and run by bodies outside the departmental framework, albeit subject to overall ministerial guidance. The proposals of the Fulton Committee were one of the catalysts for the hiving off of functions to newly created agencies. The rationales for the creation of agencies were:[9] the need to have bodies which are at arm's length from the government to carry out certain activities; the provision of expert guidance; the bringing of ordinary people into public life; the ability to respond quickly to matters which are of public concern; and the fact that such bodies facilitate a partnership between government and other interests.

More radical change was to follow, in the form of the *"Next Steps" Report*,[10] which proposed that there should be a split between service delivery and the making of policy, with a real devolution of power to executive agencies in the area of service delivery, which would cover approximately 95% of civil service activity. The report also proposed that there should be an end to the fiction that the minister was responsible for everything done by officials in his or her own name.

The Labour government continued the policy of what are now termed Executive Agencies.[11] Large parts of the civil service have been hived off and have agency status. As of June 2007 there were 86 agencies.[12] The existing mechanism for creation of an Executive Agency is as follows.[13] If following a business review the sponsor department considers that an Executive Agency is the most appropriate delivery agent, the departmental minister makes a submission to Cabinet Office and the Treasury seeking agreement to the proposals. The 'launch project' will address matters such as: the appointment of the Chief Executive, which is normally by open competition; the preparation of the Framework Document, the content of which is described in more detail below; and the preparation of an initial business plan, including key targets.

The 'map' of executive institutions in the UK has been rendered more complex by the fact that there are also what are now termed Non-Departmental Public Bodies, NDPBs, which are not Executive Agencies, but are also not part of a government department, and carry out their functions to a greater or lesser

8 *Report of the Committee on the Civil Service 1966-68*, Cmnd 3638 (1968).

9 Cabinet Office (November 1997), Chap 2.

10 *Improving Management in Government: The Next Steps* (1988); D. Goldsworthy, *Setting Up Next Steps: A Short Account of the Origins, Launch, and Implementation of the Next Steps Project in the British Civil Service* (1991).

11 Cabinet Office, *Next Steps Report 1997*, Cm 3889 (1998).

12 http://www.cabinetoffice.gov.uk/ministerial_responsibilities/executive_agencies/ This figure does not include Executive Agencies established in Wales, Scotland and Northern Ireland.

13 Cabinet Office, *Executive Agencies, A Guide for Departments* (2006).

extent at arm's length from central government.[14] There are Executive NDPBs, which are established by statute and carry out administrative, regulatory and commercial functions. They employ their own staff and are allocated their own budgets. Advisory NDPBs provide independent and expert advice to ministers on particular topics. They do not usually have staff, but are supported by staff from their sponsoring department. They do not usually have their own budget, as costs incurred come within the department's expenditure. Tribunal NDPBs have jurisdiction in a specialized field of law. They are usually supported by staff from their sponsoring department and do not have their own budgets. Independent Monitoring Boards were formerly known as 'Boards of Visitors' of the prison system. Their duty is to satisfy themselves as to the state of the prison premises, their administration and the treatment of prisoners. The sponsoring department meets the costs.

The number and range of NDPBs is significant. In March 2006 there were 883 public bodies sponsored by UK Government departments. This figure was made up of 199 Executive NDPBs, 448 Advisory NDPBs, 40 Tribunal NDPBs (counted on the basis of tribunal systems rather than individual panels), 149 Independent Monitoring Boards (previously Boards of Visitors), 21 Public Corporations, the Bank of England, 2 Public Broadcasting Authorities and 23 NHS Bodies. Executive NDPBs are probably the most important category and they carry out many important regulatory or quasi-regulatory functions in the UK.[15]

(c) Accountability for the Exercise of Executive Power

It is clear therefore at least in relation to the UK that there is no way for the genie to be put back in the bottle, not in the foreseeable future at any rate. A complex range of bodies undertakes functions of a broadly executive nature, and is likely to continue to do so. The discussion in the preceding section did not moreover touch on the complexities of contracting out and the implications that this has for the 'institutional reach' of the executive.

This naturally leads to consideration of the third of the issues outlined at the beginning of this chapter: consideration of accountability for the exercise of executive functions must be fine-tuned to the particular institution regarded as part of the executive within that country. The same point can be put in a diffe-

---

[14] Cabinet Office, *Public Bodies* (2006); Cabinet Office, *Public Bodies: A Guide for Departments* (2006), Chap 2.

[15] Examples of important Executive NDPBs are the: Civil Aviation Authority; Commission for Racial Equality; Competition Commission; Health and Safety Executive; the Criminal Injuries Compensation Panel; Office of Communications; Office of Surveillance Commissioners; Gambling Commission; Criminal Cases Review Commission; Police Complaints Authority; Parole Board; Office of the Data Protection Commissioner; Arts Council; British Museum; Higher Education Funding Council; Audit Commission; Environment Agency; Legal Services Commission; Advisory Conciliation and Arbitration Service; Human Fertilisation and Embryology Authority; Economic and Social Research Council; and the Pensions Regulator.

rent way: we can all agree that the executive should be subject to some measure of legal, political and financial accountability, but the way in which these precepts are applied may well vary depending upon the particular executive institution being considered. This point can be exemplified by a brief look at the legal, political and financial accountability structure for NDPBs.

In terms of *legal accountability*, Executive NDPBs have separate legal identity and will normally be based upon statute, or on occasion the prerogative.[16] Most Executive NDPBs require legislation, in order to confer functions on the body, and also for reasons of government accounting. The empowering legislation for such bodies will normally state their composition and powers. An action for judicial review will normally be brought against the public body in its own name, if an individual feels that the agency has exceeded its powers. Actions against bodies such as the Monopolies and Mergers Commission, the Commission for Racial Equality or the Gaming Board have been brought not infrequently. The relevant minister may also be a party to any action if the applicant claims that ministerial powers granted under the legislation have been exceeded. A number of agencies have moreover been brought within the jurisdiction of the Parliamentary Commissioner for Administration.

In terms of *political accountability*, the legislation creating the NDPB will indicate the role of the minister within the particular area. Thus the Cabinet Office Guidance to Departments when creating a public body states that departments should strike the balance between enabling the minister to fulfil his or her responsibilities to Parliament, and giving the public body the desired degree of independence. The precise balance will depend on the nature of the public body's functions and on the reasons for distancing these from government.[17] It will be common for the legislation or instrument to accord the minister power over appointment and dismissal of the chairman and board members. The legislation may also, for example, allow the minister to give statutory directions to the agency, or ministerial approval may be required before certain courses of action can be taken, or before borrowing above a certain limit is allowed.[18] Control may be exercised through non-legislative techniques, such as through conditions attached to the issue of grant-in-aid, or in a formal agreement between the department and the body.[19] The NDPB will be accountable to the Minister, with the latter being responsible to Parliament. Government practice is that if a parliamentary question raises issues concerning the day to day operation of a NDPB then the relevant minister will refer the question to the Chief Executive Officer of the NDPB for a reply, and the reply will be printed. Where however the queries raised on a particular issue are numerous, or the subject of the query sufficiently sensitive and/or high profile, then a ministerial response

16 Cabinet Office, *Public Bodies: A Guide for Departments*, n. 14, Chap 3.

17 Ibid, Chap 3, para 3.1.

18 Ibid, Chap 3, para 5.

19 Ibid, Chap 3, para 3.3.

will be more appropriate.[20] Accountability for NDPBs is also secured through select committees. Departmental select committees are entitled to examine the expenditure, administration and policy of the 'associated public bodies' of the departments concerned, which is interpreted broadly to include those instances where there is a significant degree of ministerial responsibility for the body concerned.[21] Political accountability can also be enhanced from the bottom, through public participation. This is accepted by the government. The Cabinet Office guide states that "departments and public bodies should aim to consult their users and stakeholders on a wide range of issues by means of questionnaires, public meetings or other forms of consultation to ensure that they are responsive to and meeting the needs of their customers".[22] The government's Code of Practice on Consultation is to be followed in all cases. The relevant documentation stresses moreover transparency as a method of fostering political accountability.[23]

In terms of *financial accountability*, the empowering legislation will commonly specify its method of funding, require external audit arrangements, and an annual report to Parliament. More detailed monitoring of NDPBs is achieved through what are now known as 'landscape reviews', which are designed to produce better strategic alignment of objectives, improved targeting of services and customers and better governance arrangements across a department's entire delivery 'landscape'. These are complemented by 'business reviews', which are concerned with the delivery of selected outcomes, as expressed, for example, through the targets set out in a Public Service Agreement.

2 The EU

We can now consider executive power in the EU through addressing the same questions as were considered in the context of the UK: the delineation of executive functions; the identification of the executive; and accountability for the exercise of executive power.

(a) The Delineation and Contestability of Executive Functions

It is generally accepted that executive power in the EU is shared both de jure and de facto with the Commission, European Council, Council and agencies all playing some role in relation to different aspects of the executive function. It is this very fact that makes the EU such an interesting subject of

20 Ibid, Chap 8, para 5.1.

21 Ibid, Chap 8, para 5.3.

22 Ibid, Chap 8, para 4.1.1.

23 Ibid, Chap 8, para 3.

study in relation to executive power. We shall consider the institutional dimension of this regime of shared executive power in the section which follows.

It is however instructive to begin the inquiry by considering an important example concerning the delineation and contestability of the executive function in the EU. The example concerns the Commission's self-perception of its executive function within the EU. In the most general terms, the Commission regards everything that occurs after the passage of primary legislation, whether in the form of regulations, directives or decisions, as part of its executive function, with the consequence that it should retain maximum control over the 'execution' of the primary legislation. We can see this principle playing out in relation to agencies and Comitology, which will be considered in turn.

The Commission's overall vision of the regime for EU agencies has, as will be seen, been profoundly shaped by the principle articulated in the previous paragraph. The EU does not possess regulatory agencies as that term is commonly used in national parlance, and the principal legal constraint in this regard comes from the jurisprudence of the Community courts, more specifically what became known as the *Meroni* principle.[24] It will be seen that there are however political limits to the types of power that can be accorded to agencies, or that at the very least there are ambiguities and tensions within the political organs, especially the Commission, as to whether the legal limits should be relaxed.

Let us begin by making clear the nature of the legal limits. The ECJ held that a delegating authority could not confer on another body powers different from those possessed by the delegator under the ECSC Treaty. It also concluded that it was not possible to delegate power involving a wide margin of discretion. Clearly defined executive powers, which could be subject to strict review in the light of objective criteria determined by the delegating authority, could be delegated, but discretionary power, implying a wide margin of discretion could not, since it could entail replacing the choices of the delegator by the choices of the delegate, and hence bring about an actual transfer of responsibility. This rationale for limiting the type of power that could be delegated was reinforced by the concept of institutional balance. The *Meroni* principle has stood for approaching fifty years as a constitutional limit to delegation and continues to be applied in current jurisprudence.

While *Meroni* has been criticized by academics for precluding the development of real regulatory agencies that could makes rules and decisions pursuant to discretionary power, the Commission has been content with the limits imposed by legal doctrine. The official Commission view as laid down in its 2002 Communication on Regulatory Agencies is premised on the judicial status quo, complete with the limit on delegation of discretionary power that constitutes the block to the creation of real regulatory agencies. This position has been reiterated in the Commission's 2005 proposal for a Draft Interinsti-

---

24 Case 9/56, *Meroni & Co, Industrie Metallurgiche SpA v. High Authority* [1958] ECR 133.

tutional Agreement concerning regulatory agencies.[25] The 2002 document reveals the Commission's rationale for preserving this limit that transcends the dictates of formal law. The Commission has acknowledged the virtues of independence, credibility, expertise and the like as reasons for agency creation, combined with the fact that it enabled the Commission to concentrate on its core policy-making functions. This was however balanced by repeated references to the need to preserve and reinforce 'the unity and integrity of the executive function' to ensure 'that it continues to be vested in the chief of the Commission if the latter is to have the required responsibility vis-à-vis Europe's citizens, the Member States and the other institutions'.[26] The participation of agencies should therefore be 'organised in a way which is consistent and in balance with the unity and integrity of the executive function and the Commission's ensuing responsibilities'.[27] The same language recurs later in the Communication, when the Commission considers the important issue of the composition of agency boards.[28] It is this conception of the executive function that serves to explain its approach to agencies. It can accept agencies, such as OHIM and CPVO, with individual decision-making power in discrete fields. It can embrace information and coordination agencies, where it continues to have the final say. It is reluctant to create real regulatory agencies exercising discretionary power through adjudication and rule-making, since if such power could be readily delegated then the Commission's sense of the unity and integrity of the executive function vested in it would be undermined. This would be more especially so given that the agencies would have a degree of independence and that Member States would continue to exert considerable influence through membership of the administrative boards.

The same underlying principle is apparent in the Commission's approach towards Comitology: it believes that the Commission should have greater autonomy over the passage of delegated or secondary acts than is currently the case in relation to Comitology, because it believes that matters dealt with after the passage of the primary legislation fall more properly within its sphere of 'execution'. The Commission's primary goal has therefore been to dismantle the established Comitology regime, at least insofar as it entails management and regulatory committees. It has supported the *ex ante* and *ex post* constraints on non-legislative acts of the kind contained in Article 290 TFEU of the Lisbon Treaty in the hope that the Member States might then be persuaded to modify the existing Comitology oversight mechanisms for delegated regulations.[29]

---

[25] Draft Interinstitutional Agreement on the Operating Framework for the European Regulatory Agencies, COM(2005) 59 final, Art. 5(1).

[26] Communication from the Commission, The Operating Framework for the European Regulatory Agencies, COM(2002) 718 final, 1.

[27] Ibid 1.

[28] Ibid 9.

[29] *European Governance*, COM(2001) 428 final, paras 20-29; *Institutional Architecture*, COM(2002) 728 final, paras 1.2, 1.3.4; Proposal for a Council Decision Amending Decision 1999/468/EC Laying Down

The Commission's desire to have greater autonomy over this area has been apparent for some time,[30] and was an explicit feature of the White Paper on *European Governance*.[31] The key to the White Paper was the Commission's conception of the 'Community method',[32] with the Commission representing the general interest and the Council and the EP as the joint legislature, representing the Member States and national citizens respectively. This is in itself unexceptionable. It is the implications that the Commission drew from it that are contentious.

It was, said the Commission, necessary to revitalize the Community method.[33] The Council and the EP should limit their involvement in primary Community legislation to defining the essential elements.[34] This legislation would define the conditions and limits within which the Commission performed its executive role. It would, in the Commission's view, make it possible to do away with the Comitology committees, at least so far as they had the powers presently exercised by management and regulatory committees. There would instead be a simple legal mechanism allowing the Council and EP to control the actions of the Commission against the principles adopted in the legislation. The possibility of enhancing the Commission's control over delegated regulations by abolishing or amending the Comitology procedure was raised again in other important Commission documentation.[35] The Commission appears to have succeeded in this regard, judged by the wording of Article 290 TFEU, which contains no reference to Comitology type controls, these only being mentioned in Article 291 TFEU.

Now it might well be the case that some would see nothing untoward or contentious in the Commission's vision of its executive power in relation to either agencies or Comitology. We should however at the very least be aware of the 'principle' that underlies and unites the Commission's vision in these areas and subject it to critical scrutiny. The 'principle' that everything that occurs after the passage of primary legislation is to be regarded as a matter of execution, with the corollary that it should properly fall to the Commission, was the foundation for the Commission's initial opposition to Comitology and it has changed little since then. It should nonetheless be recognized that 'execution' in this formal sense can entail anything ranging from simple mechanistic imple-

---

the Procedures for the Exercise of Implementing Powers Conferred on the Commission, COM(2002) 719 final, 2; Final Report of Working Group IX on Simplification, CONV 424/02, Brussels 29 November 2002, 12.

30 C.F. Bergstrom, *Comitology, Delegation of Powers in the European Union and the Committee System* (Oxford University Press, 2005).

31 COM(2001) 428 final. The White Paper provoked a variety of critical comment, see the *Symposium: Responses to the European Commission's White Paper on Governance*, http://www.jeanmonnetprogram.org/papers/01.

32 COM(2001) 428 final, 8.

33 Ibid 29.

34 Ibid 20.

35 N 29.

mentation, to the passage of highly complex further regulatory instruments that require a balance of competing public interests. The key issue is therefore who should have responsibility for norms of this latter kind. The Commission's approach to agencies, and its opposition to real regulatory agencies, assumes that the 'unity and integrity of the executive function' means that the Commission must retain control over such regulatory choices, rather than agencies. The Commission's approach to delegated acts is premised on the assumption that the Commission should make such norms, albeit subject to the controls contained within Article 290 TFEU, which in formal terms accords the Council and EP a power of rejection, but no power to amend such instruments. This is itself based on the assumption that the primary legislative act really does elaborate with sufficient precision the objectives, values etc on which the delegated act is to be enacted.

Space precludes further treatment of this issue here. Suffice it to say for the present that the Commission's articulation of its 'executive function' raises contestable issues as to the locus of responsibility for the making of delegated regulatory choices within the EU.

(b) The Identification of the Executive

The second issue, concerning the locus of executive power, is especially problematic in the EU. Identifying the locus of executive power in the Rome Treaty as amended is a challenging task. Most nation states will have a written constitution, which will contain provisions naming the executive and stating with varying degrees of precision its powers. This will still of course leave a plethora of issues to be resolved such as the meaning of the constitutional provisions, and the extent to which they capture the reality of executive power within that state in the light of the fact that there may be agencies and the like that exercise such power.

Identifying the locus of executive power in the EU is considerably more difficult. The EC Treaty does not contain any chapter or title on the 'Executive', nor for that matter does the Constitutional Treaty or the Lisbon Treaty. What we have are Treaty provisions dealing with the Community institutions. These Treaty articles coupled with others enable one to get a pretty good idea of the disposition of legislative power within the EU, and this is so even though there are various ways in which legislation can be made. The formal Treaty provisions dealing with institutions provide much less indication of the locus of executive power, and that is before we even factor in the reality of how the system works or the existence of other Community bodies that possess a degree of executive authority.

The reality is that executive power in the EU is shared both *de jure* and *de facto*, and that the power sharing differs in relation to different aspects of the executive function. The Treaty articles must nonetheless be our starting point, before moving on to consider the reality of executive power within the EU. The major institutional players that are relevant for present purposes are the European Council, the Council and the Commission. The Treaty articles concerning the functions of each of these institutions give little help for one who is on quest to locate executive power within the EU.

The European Council comprises the heads of the Member States assisted by their foreign ministers, and the Commission President assisted by a member of the Commission. Article 4 TEU provides that the European Council shall provide the EU with the necessary impetus for its development and shall define the general political guidelines thereof. Article 202 EC states that the Council, consisting of a representative of each Member State at ministerial level, shall ensure coordination of the economic policies of the Member States, has power to take decisions, and can confer implementing powers on the Commission. We are told by Article 211 EC that in order to ensure the proper functioning and development of the common market the Commission shall: ensure that the Treaty and norms made thereunder are applied; formulate recommendations or opinions when instructed by the Treaty or when it considers it necessary; have its own power of decision and participate in the shaping of measures taken by the Council and the EP in the manner provided for in the Treaty; and exercise the powers conferred on it by the Council for the implementation of the rules laid down by the latter.

The reader who is minded to find the institutional location of executive power in the EU will not find any greater clarity in the provisions of the Lisbon Treaty, Articles 13-19 of which deal with institutions, and this is before we even begin to factor agencies in the equation.

It is clear therefore that the bare Treaty articles do not take us very far in locating executive power in the EU. The locus of executive power, both legally and factually, can only truly be appreciated by sharper focus on the different facets of the executive function. It can be accepted that the definition of executive function varies between nation states, and can itself, as seen above, be contestable. We can nonetheless identify a core set of tasks that are commonly undertaken by the executive branch of government.

The executive will usually play a central role in setting the overall priorities and agenda for legislation. It will develop the policy choices. The executive will have responsibility for the effective implementation of agreed policy initiatives and legislation. It will normally have principal responsibility for foreign affairs and defence. The executive will have an important say in the structure and allocation of the budget. It is only by focusing on each of these in turn that we are able to identify the institutions that exercise executive authority in the EU.

This detailed task cannot be undertaken here,[36] but it is clear that under the Nice Treaty and under the Lisbon Treaty these different executive tasks will be performed by a different 'blend' of actors, and their precise role and relative power, de jure and de facto, will vary as between different aspects of the executive function.

36 P. Craig, 'The Locus and Accountability of the Executive in the EU', in Craig and Tomkins, n. 1, Chap 11.

(c) Accountability for the Exercise of Executive Power

It follows from the preceding analysis that just as in the case of the UK, so too in the case of the EU, we must focus initially when making judgments about accountability on the particular institution or institutions that are wielding executive power, and evaluating how far they comply with precepts of legal, political and financial accountability. Deidre Curtin[37] and Bruno de Witte[38] in this volume have provided valuable insights in relation to the Council and European Council respectively, and I have considered elsewhere the legal, political and financial accountability of EU agencies.[39]

There is no doubt that the new institutional ordering contained in the Lisbon Treaty will contain novel challenges in this respect, in relation to the Council, European Council and High Representative. This is in part because the relevant Treaty provisions in the TEU and TFEU are themselves complex. It is in part because it will only be with the effluxion of time that we will know how the relevant actors exercising executive power evolve and interrelate. This is especially true in relation to the new long-term Presidency of the European Council, and the High Representative, which embody novel institutional forms for the exercise of executive power.

The provisions of the Lisbon Treaty will provide the foundations for the inter-institutional disposition of executive power, but the substance will perforce be provided by the political interaction between the relevant players, whether this is in the context of planning the overall policy agenda, the execution/implementation of that policy, foreign policy, defence or the budget. The Community courts will moreover play a role, as they have done in the past, in fashioning and shaping the precepts of accountability in the new order, assuming that the Lisbon Treaty is duly ratified. It will be for the Community courts to reflect on and protect the institutional balance that underlies the disposition of executive power within the new order and where necessary intervene so as to safeguard its constituent elements.

---

37 D. Curtin, 'The Council of Ministers: The Missing Link?', Chap 12.

38 B. de Witte, 'Executive Accountability under the European Constitution and the Lisbon Treaty', Chap 13.

39 P. Craig, *EU Administrative Law* (Oxford University Press, 2006), Chap 5.